The
POWER
O F
JUDYISM

The
POWER
O F
JUDYISM

Judy Tenuta

HarperPerennial
A Division of HarperCollins*Publishers*

FIRST EDITION

Designed by Ruth Kolbert

Library of Congress Cataloging-in-Publication Data

Tenuta, Judy.
  The power of Judyism / Judy Tenuta. — 1st ed.
    p. cm.
  ISBN 0-06-096510-X (pbk.)
  1. American wit and humor. I. Title.
PN6162.T37 1991
818'.5407—dc20   90-56431

---

91 92 93 94 95 DT/RRD 10 9 8 7 6 5 4 3 2 1

TO MY FROZEN EMBRYOS

Whom I Neglected So I Could Get to the Top

Dear Eggs,
    I hope you understand that it was only by being totally self-absorbed that I could give you the truth and love that you will never know because you do not exist. As you shiver in the innermost sanctums of my freezer, you should thank me a thousand times that you will never have to endure the pain of success, glory, and adulation of millions. Please realize that it was only by totally ignoring you that I could finally love myself to the fullest extent. Won't you share this wonderful moment with me? Remember eggs, you will always nearly be my children, at least until I have to defrost.
                    Love,
                    the mother you almost had,
                    JUUUUUUUUUUUUUDY

AND

TO MY DEAREST READERS

    We are one: We flow into the same being, we flow together always. If you sit next to me long enough, we will all get our cycles at the same time. Where do I end, and you begin? I think it's when you fork over the ten bucks, suckers.

CONTENTS

ACKNOWLEDGMENTS

Photographer Slave—William Cramp.

Drawings by "Art Slave"
Derek Drymon and "Art Goddess" Judy Tenuta.

"Our Lady of Tenuta" cover photo mural design
by Bobby Kaminsky. Artist: Aida Whitney.

Special thanks to all my photo slaves:
Emo "The Human Q-Tip" Philips
"Vaudeville" Bob Rumba
"Mr. Bigstuff" Harry Hickstein
"Jammin' " Kay Cammon
"The Woodman" Cory Woods
"Cub Puppet" Edward Brandau, Jr.
"The Living Saint" Judy Tenuta

Special thanks to:
Agent stud: Richard Krawitz, APA
Editor stud puppet and pseudo-virgin:
Craig Nelson and Jenna Hull
Publicity hogs: Glenn Schwartz and Michael O'Brien
Makeup stud: Desmond Tutu
Catering stud: Lech Walesa

Special spanks to: Bob Epstein, Kurt Luchs,
Christina Wright.

And to Kitty Kelley for teaching me to get the facts from
two eyewitnesses—Stevie Wonder and Ray Charles.

And last—to each and every person who has ever lived . . .
I humbly thank you for making me look superior.

· I ·

The

POWER

O F

JUDYISM

Foreword or Preface

(Whichever You Prefer, Pig)

DO YOU DESIRE HEALTH, POWER, WEALTH, FAME AND BEAUTY? RIGHT, TOAD, YOU'LL BE ACHIEVING THOSE IN *THIS* MILLENNIUM. JUST GIVE UP NOW, FORK OVER ALL YOUR WORLDLY POSSESSIONS, AND DISCOVER THE COWLIKE JOY AND FULFILLMENT OF BECOMING A JUDY ZOMBIE. (AS IF YOU COULD ACCOMPLISH ANYTHING *ELSE* WITH YOUR LIFE, BESIDES SELLING YOUR ORGANS TO A HEADCHEESE MANUFACTURER AND THEN RENTING YOURSELF OUT AS A YUPPIE GARMENT BAG.)

This book will give you eternal life, infinite candy-pants, and love slaves aplenty . . . by teaching you the secrets of my religion, Judyism. (By the way, it's *Judyism*, not *Judaism*. In my religion, only I get to whine.) With Judyism you can forget all about your problems by thinking about *mine* for a change, ego-ass.

Yeah, like I have time not to rule the world. I am Judy, master of space, time, and panty shields. I HAVE THE POWER TO TRANSFORM MYSELF INTO ANY LIFE FORM I CHOOSE, DEPENDING UPON WHEN MY TAXES ARE DUE. I'LL EVEN BECOME A LOW-LIFE SUBURBANITE SWINE, WEAR POLYESTER AND WATCH TV; NOT BECAUSE I LIKE IT, BUT BECAUSE I HAVE TO SHARE SOME REFERENCE POINT WITH TROLLS LIKE YOU.

Anytime a mortal has a serious problem, like he can't fit into his strawberry candypants, I play a polka on his head until his brain drains and he can do nothing but work for the Pentagon. He still can't fit into his candypants, but he no longer cares because he has achieved a much higher goal: He has become a Judy zombie, and so should you, if you want to live, pig.

Now there are a few squids who might say, "Hey Judy, how can you call yourself a religious leader?" Why not? Just because I wasn't caught in a motel room with some donkey slut? I am the one true religious leader. (Deal with it, Swaggart.) There will be no peace on earth until everyone prays to me and begs me to turn them into hog fritters.

In *The Power of Judyism,* you will learn:

1. How to lose two hundred pounds in your sleep by dreaming that you're Captain Ahab and your thigh is Moby Dick.
2. How to collect ten million dollars in death and dismemberment insurance by claiming that Ed McMahon sat on your face.
3. How to achieve manly power by opening a day-care center and then spanking the five-year-old girls for being too sexually provocative.
4. How not to be a toad (well, three out of four isn't bad).

THE LEGEND OF ME, JUDY:
THE PETITE FLOWER, GIVER GODDESS, FASHION PLATE, SAINT, EARTH MOTHER, GEISHA GIRL, BUFFER OF FOREHEADS, BLESSER OF BUNIONS, HEALER OF HERMAPHRODITES, QUEEN OF CANDYPANTS, AND EMPRESS OF ELVIS IMPERSONATORS

Look, squid, so many celebrities hand you a big fat load of crap about their boring lives by whining about how they struggled to get to the top. Like we have time for this. No, I suffered more than any mortal manatee on this planet because I had to put up with their mediocrity. Why should anyone buy an autobiography of some whale when her whole stupid life was revealed in the *Enquirer* the year before?

Because I am a total giver, I will not burden you with an account of my personal problems, I'll leave that up to my relatives who will need to make an easy buck off me after I dump them.

However, if you must have some gossip about my personal life, disregard all blasphemous reports from hack rag writers who need lies to get their trash printed, and listen to me.

MY DIVINE ORIGIN

As you know, I, Judy Tenuta, was not born. I am the Eternal Goddess, "The Aphrodite of the Accordion." Once, at the dawn of time (before Nintendo), I sprouted from the left nostril of Toadra, Goddess of the Horny Water Lily. My father, Blowhard, God of Boxer Shorts, just stood there like a troglodyte on wheels and chanted, "Right on time,

Judy, the petite flower, and her mother, Toadra, goddess of the horny water lily.

slime," as I popped out of my mom's pulchritudinous proboscis into a patch of petunias. Thus I was christened "The Petite Flower."

As an infant I plotzed on a lily pad, ate chocolate-covered whale fins, and became immortal in my spare time by taking orders from Elvis, who lives in me. By the tender age of two (that's nine hundred in squid years), I could hypnotize myself and teach my body to make its own pizza. The state realized I was learning more important skills than math or physics, so they forced me to assume mortal form and attend an all girls' punk rock school, St. Obnoxious in Bondage. I was expelled after giving Sister Godzilla a shaving mug for Father's Day.

To celebrate, the king commanded me to eat five hundred peanut-butter-and-banana sandwiches. I felt reborn and I immediately started preaching the gospel of Judyism in Chicago, City of the Big Shoulders and even bigger butts. The hog butcher for the world's press was too busy worshipping false idols to acknowledge the petite goddess, so I astral-projected to New York, where I became a Big Apple goddess overnight. (It could happen.)

Next, I was asked to do *Out of Africa*. Yeah, like I have time to sit on a rhino and rotate in Kenya while Robert Redford squints. No, no, they could not possess me, no. So I let Meryl Streep have the part. She needed the exposure. Why? Because I am a giver, and everyone else is a taker.

JUDY PERFORMANCE MYTHOLOGY

So many false idols have tried to usurp my petite flower pedestal on Mount Olympus. Let's go back in time. Once, Diesel Meter, goddess of female truck drivers, tried to make me lose my sense of humor by forcing me to join an all-female improv group called Four Unfunny Dykes and a Living Saint. Our first gig was a command performance at the White House. President Reagan's cod-piece started gyrating uncontrollably. Being the healer of hermaphrodites, I whipped out my accordion and played "To Sir with Love" on his crotch. He then sobbed, "Oh Judy, I'm sick of being a puppet for the Pentagon. Make me your sex donkey."

Diesel Meter became so jealous of Ronnie's amorous advances toward me that she paid Dork-a-lingus (underground god of sublimated libidos) to leave his cage of gerbils and disguise himself as a Highland steer to seduce me. Of course I have a great fondness for grazing animals, but even *I* know that a true bovine does not have to unzip his kilts to release his love sausage.

THE VALUE OF FRIENDSHIP

From this moment on you must give up all your friends. Remember, pig, friends are just enemies who don't have the guts to kill you.

I myself have only one good friend; OK, he's an acquaintance; all right, he's a big fat mutant from hell. But I like him 'cause he's got both eyes in the same socket and he's so much fun at the airport because of the metal plate in his head.

MY REAL AMBITION

Even though I am a major cult figurine, I just want to be a wife and mother and bear fruit. I'm not even kidding now. I want to get puffed up by some stud sanitation worker with a prison record so I can carry his seed like a real woman or Peter Allen. But then my life would be too perfect and I'd have to dry out at the Betty Ford Clinic to deal with it.

My Incarnations

PETITE FLOWER
I am the petite flower: all men are begging to pollinate me.

GIVER GODDESS

I am the giver goddess: I divide the world between givers and takers. A taker is anyone who does not bring me canned goods. A giver is anyone who is intelligent enough to chant my name while jumping off a cliff. Here I give a vacuum cleaner to a homeless stud.

FASHION PLATE
I am the fashion plate: all men are begging to lick me.

SAINT

I am a living saint: I have the power to bleed from my hands and talk to small animals, especially critics.

EARTH MOTHER

I am the earth mother: If you need food, clothing, or babies, you must come to me. From now on, I am the only woman who can give birth. You will rent the womb of the goddess—a quarter a pop.

GEISHA GIRL

I am the quintessential geisha girl (suffer, Michael Jackson). Only I can give comfort to men. How? By making them feel totally worthless.

BUFFER OF FOREHEADS
I am the buffer of foreheads: Alas, poor Yorick, . . . if your skull needs shining, come to me.

BLESSER OF BUNIONS
I am the blesser of bunions. I can turn your nasty hooves into pretty paws that even Bigfoot would beg to sniff.

HEALER OF HERMAPHRODITES

I am the healer of hermaphrodites: Ask any airline steward.

QUEEN OF CANDYPANTS

I am the Queen of Candypants. Do not dare question this. You must have blind faith and eat caramel-covered corn dogs in the dark while fantasizing that your face is my pillow.

EMPRESS OF ELVIS IMPERSONATORS

I am the Empress of Elvis Impersonators. The King lives in me. He appears to me in my Cheez Whiz and says, "Priscilla, Priscilla, make me some bacon."

· II ·

The ORIGINS

OF THE

EARTHLY JUDY GODDESS

Favorite Childhood Nightmares

Let's go back in time. Oooooooh. First of all, my parents, Jo and Caes, raised me to be an accordion-playing nun. I have six brothers and one sister. Okay, I actually have one brother with six interchangeable heads. They are called "The Brothers Bosco." And their names are Bosco 1, Bosco 2, Bosco 3, Bosco 4, Bosco 5, and Bosco 6. Whenever we ate dinner it was like the Small Primate House Straps on the Feedbag. As a special treat, we'd lay down and my mom would throw lard dumplings on us.

My dad was the hot-dog soup connoisseur. He'd boil the hotdogs and we'd drink the juice. Every Saturday my dad would strap us to the kitchen table and force-feed us a

Judy, a baby fashion fox, with her parents, Jo and Caesar, and her brother Bosco 1.

pancake the size of Brazil. Then for lunch my mom would treat us to a bucket of grease and frozen fishballs. Ah, pure culinary ecstasy.

In my family, we were not allowed to laugh in the living room. We had to wait until Sunday mass, when the priest asked for money. Right, Pop, I really have a quarter for your Cadillac. I was so religious that at the dinner table every Easter I'd shout, "Jesus rose from the dead, have a chocolate egg." Then of course I had to go to confession, and of course I would confess things I did not do, because I would listen to other trolls and their sins sounded a lot better.

Once I said, "Bless me father for I have sinned . . . the Franco-Prussian War was my fault."

So then Father Shanky said, "Judy, you're sick, you need a shrink."

I said, "Right, I'm really gonna pay some Bozo fifty bucks an hour when I can talk to *you for free.*"

Even so, I had such a crush on Father Shanky. He was so cute. I used to disguise myself as my brother Bosco so that I could be an altar-ego boy. One day, in my Bosco getup, I go to our church, St. Francis of the Talking Mules, and I'm serving Mass and Father Shanky gets mad at me just cuz it was Communion time and I accidentally re-placed the wafers with real cookies. Father Shanky yells, "Why did you do that?" I said, "Come on Father, if you were God, which would you rather taste like . . . cardboard or Chips Ahoy?"

One day, I accidentally reshaped Bosco's head. Like it's my fault that he was sun-bathing while I was mowing the lawn. Then my mom got mad and said, "Judy, you're two hours late coming home from the mall. . . . And where's your brother Bosco?"

"I lost him," I said.

"Judy, how can you lose a thirty-four-year-old man at the mall?"

I said, "He bit through the harness."

Judy with her brothers Bosco 2 and Bosco 3.

Then another time I said, "Hey Bosco, if you climb to the roof of our house and jump off, I bet you can fly." But of course he broke his legs . . . cuz he wouldn't wear the towel on his neck.

Now I know you're saying, "Judy, why are you so cruel to your brother Bosco?" I am not. You see, when I was a petite kid, my mom dropped me off in the park with my oldest brother, Bosco 1. He was supposed to watch me but instead, he left me in the sandbox to die. So I was screaming my petite head off when a policeman came by and asked if I had any doughnuts, I said no, but he kept talking to me anyway. He said, "Hey little girl, are you lost?"

I cried, "No, hog, can't you see I'm in the park?"

"What's your name?" he asked. And my brother, Bosco 1, had brain-washed me into believing my name was Judy-Lynn-Pin-Marie-Tenuta-Fish.

So the guy calls my mom and says, "Mrs. Fish, we have your daughter." Not too humiliating.

Every Friday after school we had to kneel down in the living room and say the Rosary instead of watching "The Flintstones." (Nice priority skills on our part). One Friday night in mid-Rosary, I smelled smoke, so I went into the kitchen and my brother Bosco was playing with matches and I yelled, "Mom, the kitchen is on fire!"

But she was in the throws of religious fervor, her hands wildly displaying the Stigmata, shouting the Hail Mary. And she said, "Don't worry, just pray and God will take care of it."

So I went back to the Rosary and the house burned down. Then I called the fire department, just to talk, and they said, "Judy, only call if it's an emergency." Like it's not an emergency that Bosco blazes the house. I said "Bosco, why did you torch the house?"

He cried, "It was laughing at me."

I said, "Bosco, it was laughing WITH you."

Once I was riding my bike and my mom was waving to me from the window. She said, "Judy, soon your body will change."

I said, "I know—puberty."

She said, "No, that Good Humor truck."

Then I pubed out into teenhood, and my mom said, "Judy, always wear your seat belt while driving or else you'll have to paint pictures with your teeth."

You see, I have test-tube parents. They live in Chicago and buy a winter vacation home in Wisconsin. Good move, Mom. I guess you're in mensa. She says, "Judy, it's so relaxing in Wisconsin."

I say, "Mom, how much more relaxed can you get before you become a rock formation?" Like I have time to cut cheese during Octoberfest.

Only my mom would throw out a book titled *Everything You Always Wanted to Know About Anything* but save my Uncle Sloberino's ashtrays made from his clipped toenails. Perfect.

Last Thanksgiving my Anti Matter and Uncle Quark broke up our nuclear family. They shot each other over gun control. During dessert, I sat on my Uncle Guido's lap and he said, "Judy, it seems like only yesterday I was changing your diapers."

I said, "I had to pay for college somehow."

ST. OBNOXIOUS IN BONDAGE

As a petite baby goddess I was cruelly forced to attend an all-girls punk rock school, St. Obnoxious in Bondage. I don't know if we had nuns, but they wore black leather and told us the best thing to do for a non-Catholic was to knock him unconscious and then baptize him with your spit.

I hated math; I must reserve the right side of my brain for astral-projecting. But one day Sister Rotorooter got kinda moody just cuz I cracked her skull with a spitball. She said, "Judy, stand and make up a thought problem."

I said, "OK, Nun, let's say you were the only six-year-old girl on the block with a beard and a jaw like a Cheerios box. How many first graders do you have to wack with a ruler before you can join the convent? Show your work, sis."

Once my eighth-grade nun, the Demon of English, who looked like a woodchuck in a habit, made me go up to the chalkboard. I said, "Oh sister, can I please go to the bathroom? It's an emergency."

She said, "No, diagram that sentence, now." So I did and my water broke. We spent the rest of the class building

Judy shaving her eighth-grade nun, Sister Godzilla.

an Ark. Nice. Like I have time to irrigate an English class.

I'll never forget the day during religion class, when Sister Weed Wacker yelled, "Judy, time for an oral quiz," and I stuck my tongue out. She cried, "No, Judy, explain the mystery of the Blessed Trinity."

Sister Godzilla after she went AWOL from the convent.

"It's no mystery, sis," I replied. "The Blessed Trinity is a lot like the Three Stooges. You see, God the Father is mean and bossy like Moe and he yells orders out to Curly who is like Jesus. And Moe says, "Hey, muttonhead, go down to oith and save your fellow man, by hangin' on the cross." And Curly says, "But I hate nails . . . woo-woo-woo-woo-woo, nya-a-a, rruff, rruff!" And of course Larry is just like the Holy Ghost: He's around somewhere, but you never really notice him.

Then the nun poked my eyes out.

Once Sister Odor Eater caught me smoking in the lavatory. She screamed, "Judy, you're not supposed to smoke, your body is a temple." I said, "I'm burnin' incense."

So she sent me to the principal. We had this Navajo nun, Sister Spread Eagle. That was her name, I'm not kidding. (Even if it wasn't, what are you gonna do about it, toad?)

To punish me, she sent me to geography class. I loved geography because we had this really senile teacher, Mrs. Handbag. I'm sorry but this broad used to baby-sit the Redwoods. One more day and she'd be Spam. Every morning she would go up to the front of the class, open up her blouse, and shout, "Point out the Andes." I said, "Oh, I didn't know they went that far South."

She said, "Judy, you're gonna go to hell for that."

I said, "Good, we can carpool."

She said, "Judy, you don't scare me at all, I have a little girl at home just like you." I said, "Oooohhh, my dad couldn't have been that drunk."

So she called my mom. My mom said, "Judy, you're mental. Why can't you be more like your sister Blambo? She teaches special ed."

I said, "Right, Mom. Like I have time to teach jumping jacks to Republicans."

(If you are a politically love-lorn slug, call the Republican partyline. You know the number, "Dial-a-Dumbo."

As opposed to the Democratic partyline, 1-900-DON-KEYS.)

Then Mom would take me to the dentist. You know how most doctors have their credentials on the wall? Usually they have a diploma that says, PHI BETA KAI, I ATE A PIE, WHY DON'T YOU DIE? But you know what this guy has on his wall? DAVE, just DAVE in big red spray paint.

I said, "Hey, what's this DAVE stuff?"

He said, "It's my name. I want you to like me as a person. Do you like me?"

"No, but I respect you as a side of beef."

Then he's talking and there's spit foaming at the corners of his mouth. It's like these eternal rosebushes of saliva. I couldn't take it anymore, so I stuck the suction hose in his mouth and said, "If you're gonna talk, vacuum the drool, saliva smile."

To this day, I love going to the dentist, to strengthen my gums, cuz you never know when you'll have to catch a bullet with your teeth. Plus, if he gives you the right kind of filling, you can hear the FM hog report day and night. Once my Uncle Slambo was a Walnutto farmer (he grew Walnuttoes. It could happen). Anyway, he was deathly afraid of the dentist and refused to go even though he had a horrible toothache. Finally the pain was so unbearable that he whipped out a rifle and shot himself square in the kisser. I said, "Uncle Slambo, why didn't you just go to the dentist?"

Holding his bloody head he said, "What do you think I am, a masochist?"

But let's get back to my sister, whose Christian name is Varv, but that's way too weird so I call her Blambo. Anyway, for my fifteenth birthday my mom gave me these white plastic go-go boots that would make Nancy Sinatra jealous. I never took them off; I slept in those boots, until one day my sister Blambo said, "Judy, if you take off those boots, I promise not to run you over with the Chevy."

Not one to turn down a great deal, I yanked off those white plastic babies; my sister takes a deep inhale, falls off the bed and says, "Judy, you got some stanky feet. They smell like Fritos." Inspired, we go into the living room where my mom is watching TV, getting makeup tips from Lily Munster. So I whip off the boots, and my mom takes a giant whiff and yells, "Pass the Fritos." Even today, whenever there's a family squabble, I threaten them with the infamous "Frito Boots."

The Rape of My Locks

So many slugettes bow to me and say, "Juuuuuuuuuuudy, goddess of love, where did you get those lustrous locks?" Believe me when I say it's a miracle that I have any hair at all.

Let's go back in time. You see, sloths, every September from the moment I was a petite fetus, my mother would force-perm me during the Miss America pageant, hoping that I, too, would one day be crowned the Most Plastic in the Land. Right, like I have time to sing "You're a Grand Old Flag" while juggling my ovaries. Keep your legs crossed, Betsy Ross. All those beauty-pageant broads looked like Anita Bryant in a press-on wig. Also, it's really chic to Super Glue your swimsuit to your Scotch-taped buns.

One day, when I was six years old, a mere prepubescent demigoddess, my mom chained me to the high chair while my baby sister Blambo was still in it. Nice. I'm flattening my kid sister while Mom is obsessively perm-rodding me. Within two hours I was transformed into a mini Bride of Frankenstein. Imagine this frizzy-topped freak the night before my very first day of school. Perfect timing; thanks for making me into a goon, Mommy Sassoon. That morning I sat in the front yard crying my baby eyes out and Eddie Crader delivered the *Oakleaves* newspaper into my hair. At lunchtime the kids in my class hung me from my feet and whacked my hornet's head with a bat while shouting, "Where's our presents, piñata-head?"

Actually, that was a good hair-raising experience compared to the next year when she left the curling solution on during *All About Eve* and I came out looking like the Tree of Knowledge. I'm not even kidding. The neighbors would shake me for apples. I was now an ambulatory brunette bush in Buster Brown shoes. Not too humiliating.

There should be a law: "No mother can mess with her kid's curling glory." It's a crime, but until you're eighteen years old you do not have control of your own hair. So you have to pray that the woman you sprang from is not Delilah the perm-waving, meat-cleaving monster. And it wasn't just me she was hair-raising. Once a month, during her cycle, she'd line my six brothers up on the basement floor and trim them with the Toro. They looked like skinheads but not as happy. Nice scalping skills, Mom. Just to curtail their wailing, I'd let them play with my Tressy doll. They'd take turns brushing her long, blonde ponytail and watching it grow while screaming, "We hate you, you hair-teasing bitch!" That very same day, my mom took us to Sears for the family portrait. Between me, the maxipermed princess, and my Hari Krishna brothers, we looked like the Tree of Knowledge and the six gnomes with chrome domes.

That was my seventh birthday, and my mom knew that seven was my favorite number, so she hired the best children's entertainer in Oak Park. Scroto the Clown. Gooooood, Scroto. It's perfectly normal to show up for a kids party dressed in a pink tutu and a beard, wielding a chainsaw. He revved up that wild power tool and chased us around my birthday cake while singing, "Come a little bit closer, you're my kind of kids, so soft and so small."

By this time my brothers were howling their heads off in horror. They were already bald. What more could this crazed clown cut? Don't ask. Scroto kept chasing them, but he came to a dead halt when he spotted me. A little seven-year-old girl with an inhumanly huge perm. It made his multicolored rainbow wig look anemic. He stopped and stiffened in his polka-dot pants, his clown shoes flapping in the breeze, and he said, "I refuse to continue as an artist until Judy puts on a hair net. She looks like the Tree of Knowledge, for God's sake. It's a threat to my clown-hood . . . I can't even juggle . . . I can't, I can't." So my mom rips my great-grandma's Woolworth's waitress silver hair net off her head. It's okay, her coffin was still open. Then Scroto proceeded to entertain us lavishly by passing out a pack of Trojans and filling them up with water from the garden hose. Then we'd throw them at moving cars. Not too wholesome.

As night fell, he took us behind the toolshed and dug up all his former boyfriends. But just as he was unearthing the last one, wouldn't you know our next door neighbor, Officer Eatit, came over to borrow a cup of heroin, which my mom kept on top of the fridge inside the Jimi Hendrix cookie jar. Officer Eatit tripped over Scroto's shovel and said, "Hey, what's going on back here?"

Scroto said, "Oh I'm just teaching the kids about the joys of night gardening."

"But what are these bodies doing all over?"

"You know," said Scroto, "I was just gonna ask these kids that very same thing."

So then Officer Eatit turned to me and said, "Judy, do you know anything about this?"

I said, "Yeah. Scroto said, 'Let's dig up my old buddies and I'll teach you ventriloquism.' "

Suddenly his curly rainbow clown wig fell off his skull to reveal a completely hairless head. My little heart went out to him. He began weeping. I said, "Oh Scroto, don't cry just cuz you're bald and I have more hair than every Mormon combined. Think of all your other qualities."

"Like what?" Scroto asked.

I hesitated and then countered, "Well . . . for one, your talent for giving children hours of pleasure with prophylactics."

"That's true," he whimpered.

"And now you have a great future ahead of you . . . three square meals a day, and all the license plates you can press while some big Bluto on a murder wrap makes your buttocks his playpen."

My Real Dad

I'm really getting sick and tired of Frank Sinatra pretending not to be my real father. He's just too much of a baby to admit that I sprang from his crooning loins. He lets Nancy sing "Strangers in the Night"; Frank, Jr., gets to hold his sheet music; and what do I get? Accordion lessons from Stosh "the Stump." Nice one, Dad. Is it any wonder I have had to become a multimedia bondage goddess and start my own religion? Right, Ol' Blue Eyes, try to tell me I don't look exactly like Ava Gardner. It's kind of a minor tip-off that he's jealous of my success.

I'm in the audience at Bally's in Vegas. He introduces Tina and Nancy and totally ignores me and Frank, Jr. No wonder we have to get kidnapped for attention. He won't even let me open for him. No, he just sends me little notes that say, "Don't joke about me and Mia. Love, Frank."

I'll never forget the time he was headlining Caesar's Palace and Shelley Winters yelled from the back, "Hey, Frankie, sing the river song." So Dad belted out, "Rollin', rollin', rollin' on the river." So he sang all of "Proud Mary," with the Tina Turner gyrations, and got a standing ovation. But Shelley yelled out, "No, not *that* river song. The other one, you know, where the guy gets weary and sick of tryin'." My dad said, "Oh, you mean 'Old Man River.' "

Shelley yelled, "Yeah."

So Frank, Jr., handed him the sheet music and Dad threw it back and said, "Just hit it, punk. I know this mutha." What a giver.

Wanna know the real reason Frank won't admit he's the Petite Flower's pop? Wake up, squids. He's super-envious that the King lives in me. I guess Frank-O-Dad and I had a major falling out on my sixth birthday when he, Dean Martin, and Sammy Davis, Jr., jumped out of a huge whipped-cream cake in front of my first-grade class and yelled, "Judy, who is the greatest singer of all time, the King or the Chairman of the Board?"

Without hesitation I cried, "The King."

No more Rat Pack birthdays for me. Like it's my fault that the Elvis sings and the Frank-O-Dad talks.

It's true. My dad Frankie is a shower singer. I'm not even kidding. That's how he practiced every tune—in the shower. It took him eight showers a day for five weeks just to learn "My Way." The miracle was how he could fit a fifty-piece orchestra into the stall. In fact he was discovered in the bathroom of the Plaza Hotel singing "Luck Be a Lady Tonight."

Marlon Brando heard Dad in the next room and screamed, "I need that muffled swooning sound." So he jumps into Dad's shower and the next thing you know, they're in *Guys and Dolls* together. It could happen.

Pre-Goddess Jobs

Before becoming the official Love Goddess of Judyism, I too had to conform to mortal standards. One of my first jobs was as a wombat groomer for the Pet Shop Boys, but by day's end, all that wild rodent hair clung to my petite clothes and I looked like Bigfoot's wife. Plus, I had to walk past a convent after work, and of course all those cloistered nuns would salivate in unison at the sight of Mrs. Sasquatch strutting by. I couldn't have that on my conscience, so I had to quit for religious reasons.

Then I had the need to fulfill my domestic side. So I worked as a road-kill chef in Tennessee. I became quite the expert at 'possum pot pie and skunk macaroons. Truckers would come from miles around for a heaping helping of my raccoon ravioli. But then they turned the highway into Twitty City and I had to hang up the apron and bid farewell to my beloved road-kill recipes.

Like Bob Dylan says, "You may be a bartender, you may be a tennis player, but you gotta serve somebody." So I then became a candy striper at the Hinsdale Home for the Bewildered, where I tirelessly cared for octogenarians who had lost control of their bodily functions. Makes me wet just thinking about it. Once this guy who was old enough to baby-sit the Redwoods; looked like a prune with tubes hanging out of him, so you know I'm ready to walk to the altar. So anyway, I'm supposed to take his temperature, but I didn't have a thermometer, so I stuck some Sizzlean sausage on his head. Like it's my fault that it got well done.

He starts whining, "I got a fever, I got a fever, I got a fever."

So I said, "Great, are you Peggy Lee now?"

Then this other fossil's iron lung broke down. I hooked him up to my squeeze box, but he could only exhale to the "Beer Barrel Polka." And how am I rewarded for my altruism? I get fired. Nice.

But that didn't stop me from giving. I hooked up with Ma Bell as an information operator. And this guy calls up and says, "I want the number of the suicide hotline."

I said, "Okay. First, name this tune," and I played the theme from *E.T.* on the touchtone phone.

He said, "I don't know what it is . . . I want the number of the suicide hotline."

I said, "Oh, come on, you big baby, name this tune."

I play it again as he protests, "I don't know . . . I took a bunch of pills and I'm so depressed I can't find a job."

"Well, what do you do?" I asked.

He said, "Nothin'." So I said, "Try something less *competitive.*"

More and more I realized my calling as the giver goddess, so I dedicated my child-bearing years to being a surrogate mother in Poughkeepsie. Move over, Marybeth Whitehead. That pig saw what I was doing and tried to copy me. But she could not compete with the one and only "Mommy J," my code name for puffing up. The hardest part was giving up those screaming critters after they lovingly pooped nonstop into their Pampers. I had to go to Europe to forget.

I toured the British Isles as Sassy the Tap-Dancing Sloth and was a big hit until the war broke out and I had no choice but to serve my country. So I went to Nam, where Bob Hope spotted me in the front lines and signed me up for his USO tour. I became the Duchess of Da Nang until Joey Heatherton grabbed the mike and started singing, "It's Not Easy Being Green." Even I was moved.

Of course I never fully recovered from the trauma of my mother's hair abuse. So to purge myself once and for all from the fear of perm frizz, I worked as a hair sculptor's assistant at the Snip and Snatch hair salon. Right away I got reprimanded just cuz some old bat starts ranting, "I want a haircut, gimme a haircut" and I waved a hatchet in front of her puss and said, "Okay, but first tell me your blood type."

Now all of a sudden you need a stranger's permission to handcuff them to the cuticle buffer. And this one viking cleaning woman got all huffy just cuz I hung her upside down from the rotating disco ball. Well, how else am I supposed to hot-comb her pits?

The incident that caused my dismissal involved my boyfriend's mother, Anne of a Thousand Pounds. She strutted in, vibrating like a Jell-O mold in a muumuu and said, "Hey Judy, I want the hot-wax treatment. Gimme the hot wax." And then she started screaming just cuz the candle set her beard on fire. A giver never wins.

Old Flames of the Goddess

PRINCE EDWARD

Let's face it, trog, Prince Edward can't live without me. He's willing to abandon his wildly successful career as a backstage florist to be my love slave. He constantly parades the streets of London dressed like me. Well, can you blame him? He certainly can't dress like Queenie. She needs major-league miracle fashion healing from the goddess.

The queen, of course, is elated that Edward is enamored of me. Just yesterday she called me. It could happen. She said, "Juudy, will you come over and teach me to play the accordion?" I said, "Right, Queenie, like I have time to let you impersonate me on your world tour."

BUZZ ALDRIN

Buzz Aldrin is really hot for me. He's such an astronaut. He says, "Judy, I love you but I need space." I said, "Great, Moonstruck, elope with an asteroid, see if I sweat."

THE POPE

The Pope is my main squeeze. I'll never forget the time we had a major-league falling out. We both showed up at the Mr. Leather Swiss Guard Contest wearing the same gown. (Both in long white silk, only I didn't wear a plug on my head.)

The next night I caught him doing the Lambada with Mother Theresa. Of course he came back to me and took me for a spin in the Popemobile. He drove me to Poland, where he refused to use his influence to cut into the twelve-hour line for a potato, and we broke up soon afterward.

Real thoughtful, Padre.

*A*stral-*P*rojecting
with the *G*oddess

THE SOUTH

Once I was driving really far south: Alabama, Georgia, El Salvador. When you're driving through the South and you have a license plate from up north, you might as well have a sign on your car that says: STOP ME AND MAKE A FAST FIFTY, OINKER.

I'm not saying this cop was looking for a handout, but he was posing like an Egyptian hieroglyphic, and said: "Hey Judy, your car is blue, I'm gonna have to strip-search you."

I said, "Ohhhh. That sounds legal, Goober."

He said, "You're kinda sassy, missy. Yep, you're kinda sassy. Is everybody that sassy where you come from?"

I said, "Yeah, we're pretty hip on the planet Earth." This guy was going to night school to evolve a thumb. He was excess baggage in the airport of life.

Suddenly he took my license, as if to strip me of my identity. He said, "Judy, you know what's wrong with you? You got that Yankee hostility."

I said, "It's called INTELLIGENCE."

"Judy, you don't know nothin' about the South. You don't even know the difference between the North and the South."

I said, "Oh yes I do. In the North, there's a cut-off age for sleeping with your parents."

INDIANA

One day they decided to close Indiana, and the world rejoiced. It was a blessing even God had prayed for. It was the winter of '83, and I was driving back to Illinois in my fully loaded Pacer, so of course a blizzard hits. All I could see were white sheets pounding on my windshield. I had accidentally driven into a Klan meeting. (Just seeing if you were awake, ape.)

Finally a cop pulls me over and says, "Hey Judy, Indiana is closed because of the snow. You'll have to sleep with the National Guard." Great. So nine months later I get a phone call saying I'm the mother of Indiana, and now they want hog-imony.

Don't get me wrong—Indiana is a nice place if you're a corn husk. It's in the North, but they think they're from the South. They talk like they're from Alabama; I'm not even kidding.

Like once I was driving through Indiana in my YugoFaster, when suddenly the highway ends and turns into a Suzuki shop. So I go inside, and there's a couple who look exactly like *American Gothic*.

I say, "Could you please tell me what happened to the expressway? Why is it a Suzuki shop?"

They say, "Judy, we're tard, we're just tard."

I say. "Put a 're' before the 'tard' and you'll be accurate."

Then I stay in their motel and they say, "Hey Judy, do you want us to put your calls through?"

I say, "Oh no, just bash in my door at two A.M. and act them out."

So I'm in the gift shop because maybe I need a keychain, do you mind, toad? So I'm trying to buy a key chain and Ma and Pa Kettle say, "Oh no, Judy, don't get a keychain . . . what you need is a rifle."

I say, "Aren't guns dangerous?"

"Oh no, lots more people are killed by cars than by guns."

So I robbed them with a sawed-off Pinto.

TEXAS

Now, let's astral-project to Texas, one of my favorite countries in the world. That's right, love-hog, Texas is a country. As soon as you cross the state line, if you're not wearing a ten-gallon hat and cowboy boots, you're hung as a spy from Pansyland. In the middle of every mall is a rodeo, where you can lasso your own steer and turn him into four-alarm chili after you've dated him.

TOAD SUCK, ARKANSAS

First of all, it's just the best name ever: Toad Suck, Arkansas. Home of my favorite kind of hog: the Razorbacks. In this town, you're born, suck on an empty beer bottle until you sound like a toad in heat, go to a tractor pull, and die. Ecstasy, thy name is Toad Suck.

PROVIDENCE, RHODE ISLAND

If you really want to tower over the townsfolk, go to Providence. At 5'4", I'm the tallest woman in Rhode Island and I don't even live there. I mean it. As you stroll the streets, you see that every broad looks like a fire hydrant with a bouffant, holding a tray of rigatoni.

BOSTON, MASSACHUSETTS

To feel verbally superior, go to Boston. They all sound like they're three years old. To carry on a conversation you have to talk like a toddler. They're into preschool-speak. It's a mortal sin to pronounce your r's. I'm not even kidding. You'll always hear them say, "Pock da cah." And those are the congressmen. It's called the Cradle of Liberty because everyone there talks like they're still in diapers. Oh Boston, my Boston, keep babbling that babytalk and save me some "Chowda," you hot scrods of lust.

SANTA MONICA, CALIFORNIA

Now let's time-travel to La La Land, where all the alfalfa-snouts are channeling yucca plants. So I'm walking with the mayor of Santa Monica, and he says, "Hey Judy, you don't think we have too many homeless people, do you?"

I say, "Oh no, it's perfectly normal for the sidewalk to be soft." I felt like Scarlett O'Hara tripping over bodies on the Civil War field.

SEATTLE, WASHINGTON

I'm not saying this place is inhabited by mountain mutants, but all the residents answer to "Babe the Blue Ox." I love Seattle's slogan, "The best kept secret in America," hoping that out-of-state humans will be tricked into their gene pool. Yeah, they're almost used to civilization.

So good, I love it, I'm strolling fifty blocks away from the nearest department store, the Annie Oakley Holistic Feed Post, and the saleslady senses my potential purchasing vibes, propels herself through the display window like the Road Runner possessed, grabs me by the neck, and screams, "Can I help you?" I'd say *you* need the help, Miss Desperato. Not toooo hyper. Did you OD on the Frankenberry?

CANADA

I love to drive into Canada because you get to go through customs at the border. And there's always a very sweet customs officer on duty. Now I don't want to talk about this broad, but at least when I walk down the street, people don't pull in their young. I almost believe this babe had a female hormone. She looked like Ernest Borgnine's illegitimate stepnephew.

So she breaks open my luggage with her jaw and smashes my deodorant to pieces.

I say, "I realize that stuff is foreign to your parts, but we use it in the United States."

"Well, we have to check you Americans cuz lots of times you guys try to stay up here in Canada, eh?"

I said, "Count on it, Dudley-Do-Dyke. It's eighty below in Canada even in July. The only reason we would ever come up here is the war in Vietnam . . . and IT'S OVER."

She said, "Okay, so why did you come up to Canada, eh?"

I said, "For your ginger ale."

And then I made eight fur coats out of her unwanted hair.

THE NEW PROMISED LAND

So I'm on this airplane. I didn't have to go anywhere, I just needed a great meal, a good night's sleep, and a flying out-house propelling through space at 350 miles an hour. So anyway, sitting next to me is this miniature motormouth. He says, "Hi, I'm Jacob."

I'm thinking, "Great. Where's Manson when you need him?"

But the kid is so excited and keeps talking and says, "You know, this morning I went to Temple."

I say, "So why weren't you sacrificed?"

He says, "The Rabbi told us that God got really mad at the Jews after they built a great big Golden Calf so He made them leave Israel and go far away."

"Where did He make them go?"

He thinks for a minute and says, "To Florida."

Dogma on Comedy

Comedy is the AIDS of the nineties. I'm not saying there are too many comics, but I'm on the operating table at Illinois Moronic Hospital, having my petite flower giver goddess appendix removed, and the surgeon says, "Hey Judy, I want you to listen to my tight five on talking cars."

I say, "No thanks, Mucous Welby, they already gave me anesthetic."

I now officially declare it my duty as the Goddess of Orkin to exterminate all cockroaches who have quit their jobs as armpit sniffers to be regulars on the Yuk and Suck network.

But if you absolutely *must* be a comic, because you were inspired by me, then you must follow the Goddess's

FIVE COMMANDMENTS OF COMEDY

1. Make the audience feel needed. Tell them they are just useless globs of carbon molecules trying to impersonate life.
2. Seize the moment. Let's say you're doing your act (which is unusual, since most comics do mine), and the building suddenly blows up. Why not improvise and say, "Hey, was that a bomb, or what!?" Then sit back and wait for the howls.
3. Join an improv group. That way you don't have to be funny, or even have a reason to live, unless the audience yells one out.
4. If an audience is unusually quiet (or, as I would say, hopelessly stupid), try something different, like telling a joke.
5. If all else fails, learn to juggle.

COMICS I ADMIRE

I really admire female comics who open their acts by saying, "I'm single, unmarried, divorced, dating, and I wear a pad." But even more, I admire male comics who do a tight ninety minutes on tampons and then get their own shitcom.

Once my opening act, Tommy Hack (now star of the hit TV series "Full Pants"), was driving me through the Badlands of South Dakota. He said, "Hey Judy, what do you think of my act? Be honest, what do you really think?"

I said, "Ask me again when we get a little closer to town."

PIGS IN POWER

Some psychopath with an ax breaks into the Warner Bros. Film Vault and starts chopping up all the funniest films of the century. Instead of arresting him, they make him president of the Yuk and Suck channel.

Then he says, "Judy, we have revolutionary programming as well. We've just purchased all 60,000 episodes of 'The Mary Tyler Moore Show.'"

Good, Che Guevara. As if I'm not already picking them up on Channel 50, Nickelodeon, and my step-nephew's butt braces.

ATTEMPTS TO CENSOR THE GODDESS

So I'm doing the Diet Dr Pepper commercials, and everything is going great, and then the pig censor waddles onto the set. She's a five-thousand-pound Teamster in a mini-dress. She says, "Hey Judy, you're not supposed to say 'power tool.'" (Like I was even thinking of it.) She says, "You can't say 'power tool,' it's offensive to middle America."

Meanwhile, you guys are trying to eat dinner, and they keep showing these commercials about feminine plumbing products. You know, where the mother and daughter are on a swing in the woods (that could happen) and the daughter says, "Oh Mom, I feel so close to you." And the mom says, "Good, stick this in your pants."

*A*uthentic
*E*nglish *T*heater *Q*uiz

(for no reason at all)

Match the following great quotations
to the Legendary British actors
who said them.

1. Lord Laurence Olivier
2. Dame Edith Evans
3. Sir John Gielgud
4. Dame Glenda Jackson
5. Sir Ralph Richardson
6. Dame Maggie Smith
7. Sir Richard Burton
8. Dame Vanessa Redgrave
9. Sir Charles Laughton

a. "Just try to upstage me, sea cow."
b. "Right hog, like you almost have a reason not to throw yourself off the White Cliffs of Dover."
c. "Nice acting skills, ape-in-waiting."
d. "Excuse me, gerbil-master. Keep your bloody nose putty out of my pork pie."
e. "This butt plug's not for burning."
f. "When in doubt, be a hunchback."
g. "Oh I'm shakin', Francis Bacon."
h. "I may be a great Richard the Third, but I'm no Judy Tenuta."
i. "Heathcliff, oh Heathcliff, give me a ride on your Canterbury tail."

The Day Detroit Devoured My Wardrobe

Okay, so this is not too perfect. I'm in Detroit trying to leave my hotel to catch a flight, and I can't go because the Haitian maid has sold my clothes to a fan who slipped her fifty bucks while I was in the shower. *Nice!* Like my goddess gowns aren't worth twice as much.

I now have twenty minutes to get to the airport and I'm totally nude. It's eighty below outside so I safety-pin two Holiday Inn towels together to cover my petite bod and I board the plane wearing a parka and a terry cloth towel muumuu. The Barbie-doll stewardess says, "Where are you going dressed like that?"

I say, "I'm going to Hawaii by way of Alaska. Do you mind, flying floozie?"

To which she counters, "I'm sorry, ma'am, but you are not properly attired to sit in first class."

Desperate, and near tears, I say, "Look, I'm Judy Tenuta, the Petite Flower, and while I was taking a shower in my hotel room the maid sold all my clothes to a fan, so I had to do some fashion improvising."

She yawns, unimpressed, and replies, "Right, honey, and I'm Mother Theresa."

Just then this guy struts onto the plane dressed in my gold lamé goddess cape, complete with flower in his hair. The Barbie stewardess sees him, does a double take, and faints. As I'm about to tell him off for not paying full price for my divine duds, he takes my hand, kisses it, and says, "Miss Tenuta, it's an honor to have you on board, Captain Crosser at your service." He then bows, goes into the cockpit, and flies the plane. *It did happen!*

Letters
to the Living Saint

Dear Fashion Plate,
   Where do you get those wonderfully wild and wacky goddess gowns?

A Fellow Fashion Fox,
Elton John

Dear Elton,
   Check your closet, Rocketman.

o   o   o

Dear Judy,
   As a heavenly being, do you also have an earthly birthday that we all can celebrate?

Sincerely,
The League of Nations

Dear League of Nations,

Yes, I was born on November 7th, the same day as the Bolshevik Revolution. Which means that I have the same biorhythms as Russia. So every twenty-eight days, I get the overpowering urge to invade Poland.

o   o   o

Dear Princess of Perfection,

Do you have an earthly residence?

Love,
Carl Sagan

Dear Carl Sagan,

Yes, when I'm not astral-projecting, I live in Oak Park, Illinois, which is also the home of Ernest Hemingway and Frank Lloyd Wright. So I like to sit in uncomfortable chairs and shoot moose.

o   o   o

Dear Judy,

Is there anything about love relationships that you hate?

Love,
The Gay Bowlers of America

Dear Gay Bowlers,

You know what makes me sick? When two people fall in love and get married just because they had a few kids. Then they call me up to baby-sit and since I hate the brats, I say, "Sure."

So I'm baby-sitting the clap twins, "Herpe and Slurpee." And I have to put them to sleep for their own good. So I take them to their room and turn off the light and they scream, "Judy, we're scared of the dark, we see monsters on the chairs." I say, "No, those are just your clothes . . . trying to murder you." Yeah, I'm really good with toddlers.

Dear Countess of Comedy,
   Why do so many comedians go on the tube and brag, "As a comic I do a lot of traveling?"

Snatchy O'Malley

Dear Snatchy,
   If you got kicked out of every town you ever played in, you'd keep moving too.

Dear Judy,
   What advice can you give to an up-and-coming performer who wants to make it big in show business?

Love,
Pat Sajak

Dear Pat,
   Shave your head, roll naked in a music video with a negro saint, grow Rasta braids, grab your crotch, and lip-sync to Roseanne squealing the national anthem.

The Emergency Room

Why is it that every time you go to the emergency room with a trick knee, you leave with AIDS? No really, you waddle up to the registration desk needing only a splint and an aspirin, but you end up on a life-support system. Why? Because all the other scrotum in the waiting room are bleeding all over you.

One February night, I'm doubled over in pain because my ovaries are doing a triple sow-cow, and I'm on the subway with Hell's Angels. Perfect. So by the time I reach the St. Joseph's Baby Aspirin Hospital, I'm holding my severed head in a glass of milk. The emergency room nurse is really sensitive. She says, "What seems to be the problem?"

I say, "Oh, no problem, sea cow. I want to start a New Wave band. You know, 'The Talking Heads.' "

Astute as ever, she replies, "Are you sure you're not pregnant?"

Shaking my bloody skull with both hands, I say, "Yeah, anal nitrate queen. I'm Zeus and the kid is gonna sprout from my neck. It could happen."

She sees the blood gushing from the stump where my head used to be and says, "Oh that's some little cut you've got there, missy," and valiantly hands me a Band-Aid.

All you stud puppets and virginettes should only pray that you're never in an accident . . . besides birth. Especially if you have no insurance, you're in a complete body cast, and your family is now "Kibbles and Bits." You're in the emergency room and Nurse Hatchet says, "Well, it could have been a lot worse."

I say, "Yeah, I could have died and come back as you, Freida Kreuger."

So now, just as the sun is about to burn out, the doctor enters the examination room and says, "OK, Judy, lay down."

I say, "Buy me a drink first, pig."

Then he whips out a needle the size of a cruise missile, aiming right for my petite derriere, and he says, "You'll feel a slight pinch." Oh, thanks for the warning, Cape Canaveral.

After a moment's contemplation he says, "I'll have to remove everything from your waist down."

Startled, I say, "But what's wrong with me?"

He smiles and says, "Oh, you're fine, but I need a new Porsche."

He then hangs up his butcher's apron and says, "I'll have to operate tomorrow morning because today is Wednesday and I'm in the middle of a golf game."

"Come on, scrod, you can hit the ball through the clown's mouth anytime."

The next day all that's left of me is a torso in a hospital tunic. My friends come to visit and they really know how to cheer me up. Even my ninth-grade nun, Sister Led Zeppelin, says "You know, Judy, now that you're just a midsection, you're so lucky. You no longer have to bear the burden of a whole mortal body."

I say, "Right, it's so liberating to know I can work exclusively in a Greek restaurant as a souvlaki on a spit. And all my fans can just grab a piece of me."

Suddenly I have a flashback, all the way back to the time I was an embryo. The doctor had left a sponge in my mother's womb so I had an agent since birth. He too comes to visit me. His name is Murray Embezzleschnoz, and he says, "Kid, you got a great future ahead of you. . . . No one, not even Streep, can compete with you now. I got you a bit part in *Glory II*. You'll play the unknown torso that Ulysses S. Grant stumbles over on the battlefield. Then you'll costar with Arnold Schwarzenegger in his newest flick, where you'll both become buddy cops, trade torsos, and arrest June Allyson for selling retirement diapers. It's called *The Terminator Twins*."

Then it suddenly hits me. I say to myself, Judy, you really are fortunate. When you were a whole woman you had to beg for everything you ever got in this damn stinkin' business they call "show." Now the tables are turned and all the bigwigs want the hot Tenuta Torso. Well grovel, goons.

Goddess Gossip Scoops

So I'm backstage at the White House correspondents dinner, and Charlton Heston comes up to me and he says, "Hey Judy, I used to play the accordion, too."

I say, "Right, like Moses had a squeezebox."

Okay, that would have happened, if I did the White House correspondents dinner in March of '89 like I was supposed to. See, the CIA of entertainment contacted me in November of '88 to say, "Hey Jude, please abuse all the newscasters at the White House correspondents dinner." Peter Jennings, what a hot hairball of manhood. And, of course, Dan "I'd Rather Be in Philadelphia." And Sam "I'm the risk-taking man" Donaldson. So I'm getting all revved up to do the dinner, but then the Supreme Court review board decides that I might spit my gum in Bab's Bush or make George squeal like a lovesick sow, so they paid me $5,000 not to come. It's like I'm a farmer and the government is bribing me to plant my jokes underground. Is it any wonder that I'm kinda moody?

Then of course I went to London to do a Bondage Mime show for Prince Edward. I'm sorry, this guy might pass for straight, but it wouldn't take much of a prison term to make him switch over. Like a parking ticket would do it. So anyway, the Queen comes up to me (she looks like a muffin with feet) and she cops a major attitude. She says, "Hey Judy, gimme six bucks for Spam."

I say, "Wait a minute. You're the Queen of England. What are you doing asking me for money?"

She says, "Judy, just shut up and fork it over." And just as I was whipping out my petite wallet, Fergie comes flying into the room on Budgie the Helicopter and the Queen's water broke.

So then I fly back to New York to do "Night of 100 Stars," and backstage Katharine Hepburn is doing the Funky Chicken with Jimmy Stewart, and believe me, I haven't seen that many celebrities since I was parking cars at the Betty Ford Clinic. And for the grand finale, the Golden Girls had a séance to try to bring their periods back.

Celebrity Feuds

SONNY BONO

Okay, I guess Sonny Bono is kinda moody just because I was supposed to do "Friday Nite Videos" with him, and the director and myself, the Petite Flower, thought it would be great for me to dress up like Cher so that Sonny could have a function. So Sonny shows up on the set with his new future wife, who, for the first time, does not look like Cher. Remember when he married all those other babes who were like Ukrainian Easter dolls of Cher? You open one up and there's another one inside who looks just like the one before it, except smaller in mind and body. But this time Sonny prances in with the new fiancée, who is fresh out of the Roman Polanski Day Care Center. She's still teething, okay, trolls?

Anyway, I walk up to them in my full Cher garb and start singing, "If I could turn back time . . . I would date a fetus."

Sonny starts screaming, "I'm having a flashback! It's Cher. Cher, I've got you, babe." And then he passes a water bill in his pants. He tells the director he didn't want to be the straight man. Like that could ever happen. Fat chance, Sundance. This trog is Cher's coatrack for twenty years and then decides when he meets the Love Goddess of Comedy that he's Harpo Marx. Fantasize, Mayor Bellbottom Bono.

BOB COSTAS

And how about Bob Costas? I taped "Later" with him and they said, "Go wild, Judy." So I sat next to him, gave him a mini squeeze box so we can play a duet, and he claims that I was too wild, that I was all over him. He wishes. I guess it's my fault that I have a pulse and that I'm not sitting there crying about how I reached nirvana at a detox center. Is it so wrong for me to be a living saint and not a whining wildebeest?

Then Bob asked, "How can I become a Love Slave?"

I said, "Put on this stud-puppet safe-sex cap and breakdance." And he didn't even stage a micromini protest. He was too willing. So then I sat on his sportscaster's lap for five seconds and can I help it if his dolphin started dancing?

Of course he could not control himself. I am the Love Goddess. I can make mere men put on aprons and can red beets. The ironic part is that the following year, I went to

Washington, D.C., to tape "Larry King Live" and Bob Costas, his big pal, comes backstage to tell me he wants me to tape another "Later" show with him. I said, "Perfect, so you can hide it in the Al Capone vault for Geraldo?"

Then he egged me on big-time to torment Larry King. He handed me blow-up dolls and said, "Go nuts." I did, and Larry was the quintessential great sport puppet. He even put a pig nose on.

Come on, Costas. You know you can't wait to put bread in my oven, you hot little mule muffin.

THE POPE

John Paul, that is. I guess you all know by now that I'm dating the Pope. OK, I'm just using him to get to God. He is a fashion plate. But now he's mad at me just because we showed up at this celebrity drag race wearing the same gown. Like it's my fault that we're both drop-dead gorgeous in long white silky dresses. Besides, I'm kinda huffy about the fact that he wanted Madonna to tour with him—that mattress with a microphone. That false idol with brass nipples. I hope she has another hit movie this year, "Desperately Seeking Talent," costarring my favorite rock star, La Toilet Jackson.

Once I was in Rome for a pasta convention and the Pope didn't even pick me up in his souped-up Popemobile. Like I'm gonna ignore that snub. So to cheer myself up, I went to Monaco, where Princess Stephanie taught me how to pick up disco dorks by wearing a crew cut and a G-string stuffed with megabucks.

MISS GUATEMALA

I was on this talk show with Miss Universe, formerly Miss Guatemala. She kept saying, "You know, Judy, I don't date, I do not date during the contest."

I said, "No, you don't date. You just lay down and wait to get graded." I guess we won't be sharing Maxithins. I'm sobbing.

· IIII ·

Judy's

INTERVIEWS

WITH THE

STARS

*M*arlon *B*rando

JUDY: Mr. Brando, you were considered the major screen stud of the twentieth century. So why did you blimp out?

MARLON: [Oblivious to my question] I'm starving. Do you have any fried grease?

JUDY: Not on me. Now back to your movie career. One of your greatest films was *On the Waterfront*. You coulda been a contender. So why did you eat yourself into oblivion?

MARLON: Pass the lard. [Burp, belch]

JUDY: Oh, nice self-control, Bluto. Let's talk about your astronomical fees. Why did you get four million bucks to appear for ten minutes as Superman's dad?

MARLON: I needed the money for . . .

JUDY: Say it. You needed the money for fooooooooooood.

MARLON: Just shut up about my eating habits.

JUDY: Fine. Let's talk about your costars. Is it true that you are feuding with Eva Marie Saint to this very day just because she stole your deli tray?

MARLON: Stop it. Stop it, I tell you. I can't take it anymore.

JUDY: OK, you're right, I apologize, Godfather. That was another landmark film for you. The entire world loved you and yet we couldn't understand a word you said.

MARLON: Yeah, I kinda mumble. That's how I talk—it's my style.

JUDY: No, wait a minute. I just realized that's not how you really talk. You've been mumbling through all your films because your mouth is full of fooooooooooood. [He puts me in a headlock and uses me for a human jack-hammer.] No wait. I meant it as a compliment. Keep eating, always stuff your face. You gotta keep that Brando voice mumbling forever. . . . Are we friends?

MARLON: OK. But no more talk about you know what.

JUDY: Right. So you bought an island. Why?

MARLON: I want to be left alone.

JUDY: Right, Greta Garbo. Are you sure it's not because you're a big blob who can only play a volcano in your next film?

Barbara Walters

JUDY: Barbara, if you could be a vegetable, what kind would you be? Not that you have far to go . . .

BARB: Weww, wet's see . . . umm, I guess I'd wike to be bracowee.

JUDY: What the hell is bracowee? Oh, you mean broccoli.

BARB: Yeah, that's what I said. Bracowee. I'd just wuv to be bracowee.

JUDY: Why? So George Bush wouldn't eat you?

BARB: No, so I could be covowed in howwondaze.

JUDY: Babs, it's not howwondaze. It's hollandaise.

BARB: Wight. Howwondaze.

JUDY: Repeat after me, Eliza. The rain in Spain stays mainly in the plain.

BARB: The wain in Spain stays mainwee in the pwain.

JUDY: Good. It's kind of a hint that you swallowed Elmer Fudd.

BARB: I wewe wesent that; what Elmur and I had was sakewed. [She breaks down and cries.]

JUDY: Come on, Babs. You know better than to cry during interviews. Besides, Elmer Fudd was just a cartoon character. [She starts hitting me with her purse.]

JUDY: Cool it, Ruth Buzzi.

BARB: Elmur was the ownwee weeol man I've evawe known.

JUDY: You mean you and he did the "wild thang"?

BARB: Yes. Evwee night Elmur would whip out his jackhammew and dwiw me wike a New York City sidewalk.

JUDY: Babs, please restrain yourself.

BARB: I can't. I'm wewe awouzed.

*M*arie *A*ntoinette

JUDY: So did it hurt or what?

MARIE: What? Did what hurt?

JUDY: Only the most painful thing in your life.

MARIE: Oh, sleeping with my husband, Louis?

JUDY: No, squid. The guillotine.

MARIE: Oh that. Well, kind of. But it was nothing compared to that damn royal corset I had to be poured into just to flaunt my hourglass figure.

JUDY: You mean the Empress Marie Antoinette didn't like dressing up?

MARIE: It's OK for weddings and stuff, but I'd much rather lounge around in my tube top and Calvin Kleins.

JUDY: They didn't have Calvin Kleins back then.

MARIE: Listen, honey, with my money I could get what you can only dream about.

JUDY: Yeah, well, try buying yourself a head. Guess you can only dream about that.

MARIE: You bitch.

JUDY: So I'm the bitch, am I? Just try interviewing a dead queen with no noggin, Miss "Let them eat cake."

MARIE: I never said that. Everyone thinks I did. But I didn't.

JUDY: Well, who did say it, Sara Lee? Now I suppose you're gonna tell me that you never had sex with a horse.

MARIE: I didn't. That was Catherine the Great.

JUDY: Right, headless horse humper. See you next Halloween.

Julius Caesar

JUDY: Hail, Caesar.

CAESAR: Hail, Judy, full of jokes.

JUDY: You mean that you, Julius Caesar, recognize me?

CAESAR: Of course. You're Judy the Petite Flower, Giver Goddess, fashion plate, and founder of your own religion, Judyism.

JUDY: Yeah, yeah, but don't you notice any resemblance between yourself, the great Emperor of Rome, and me, the Empress of Elvis Impersonators?

CAESAR: No, should I?

JUDY: Oh, nice attitude, your Romanness. I suppose you're also gonna deny that you are my real father.

CAESAR: How could I possibly be your father? I was alive 40 B.C. and you weren't born until the middle of the twentieth century A.D.

JUDY: Likely story, your squidness. I am a goddess. I am ageless. I lived then as I live now, and forever. Besides, look at my birth certificate. My father's name is Caesar.

CAESAR: It says your father's name is Caesar Tenuta. I am Julius Caesar.

JUDY: Like there's a difference, scrod. We all know you dropped "Tenuta" and tacked on "Julius" for show-business reasons.

CAESAR: Show business? I'm not in show business. I am the greatest emperor of all time. I am not related to you in any way.

JUDY: Oh, right, like it's a coincidence that we are both wearing long white togas and wreaths in our hair.

CAESAR: Look, that's how a Roman emperor dresses.

JUDY: Oh, real masculine, Caes. You know you're dressed this way because you want to be me; to be showered in rose petals and bathed in donkey's milk by beefy burritos of manhood.

CAESAR: You have beefy burritos?

JUDY: Of course, and they lick the sleep from my eyes every morning and, furthermore, they don't gang up on me and stab me fifty-two times just cuz I'm a tyrant.

CAESAR: Oh, wicked fate. Did you have to bring that up? And I was not a tyrant.

JUDY: No, it's perfectly normal to roll on the floor and turn blue until you get your way, you big baby. And besides, you never took me to a baseball game. For your information, in May 1989, I was in the broadcast booth at Shea stadium with Tim McCarver doing play by play.

CAESAR: Tim McCarver, the catcher for the Saint Louis Cardinals?

JUDY: Yeah, and I called Sid Fernandez a love hog.

CAESAR: Wow.

JUDY: And Tim McCarver was chanting "It could happen." Where were you, Dad?

CAESAR: I was dead.

JUDY: Like that's ever stopped anyone from getting what they wanted. Look at Hamlet's dad; he visited his kid.

CAESAR: That's true, but . . .

JUDY: Yeah, and how about the time I got a standing ovation at the very beginning of my show from over ten thousand sailors in 1983?

CAESAR: How'd ya do that?

JUDY: I just got onstage, pointed to the only officer in front and said, "Are you the Captain?" He said, "Yes, I am." And I said, "Hey, sailors, what do you say I discipline this pig?" The whole place went mental for five minutes.

CAESAR: Gee, I wish I could get that reaction from my senate.

JUDY: Fat chance, Julie.

CAESAR: Don't call me Julie. I hate that. Brutus called me that.

JUDY: Sorry, Caes. I guess you must be pretty sore about Cleopatra, too.

CAESAR: Oh, great. You really know how to hurt a guy. I could have had her if it wasn't for that damn Richard Burton.

JUDY: Yeah, how are you supposed to top him in the romance department? But at least you were tops as a tyrant.

CAESAR: You really think so?

JUDY: Except for maybe Hitler or Stalin.

CAESAR: Who the hell are Hitler and Stalin?

JUDY: Gee, Dad, you are out of it. How about if I play you a special song on the accordion?

CAESAR: You play the accordion? I can't believe it. I play the accordion too. I do a great "Lady of Spain." Let me play, would you?

JUDY: OK, but only if you kiss my feet, take me to the vomitorium, and promise to be my dad from now on.

CAESAR: Deal.

Edward VII, Duke of Windsor

JUDY: You abdicated the throne of England to marry Wallis Simpson.

EDWARD: Yes, I did.

JUDY: So, Edward, are you happy that you traded your kingdom for a horse?

EDWARD: How dare you call my wonderful Wallis a horse. She was not a horse; she was a splendid, beautiful woman.

JUDY: Right, Mr. Ed. Then how come every time there was a diamond brooch within a twelve-mile radius, she would break into a trot?

EDWARD: The Duchess was very athletic. That is all.

JUDY: Yeah, like it's perfectly normal for Parliament to place bets whenever she'd walk through a gate.

EDWARD: I will not have you talk that way about the woman I loved. She was a lady and an elegant dresser.

JUDY: She looked like a tax attorney in drag.

EDWARD: That's exactly what I liked—I mean, she did not. She was very feminine.

JUDY: Yeah, for a truck mechanic. She must have been a great lay.

EDWARD: Whatever do you mean?

JUDY: Come on, Princey, do I have to draw you a map? She must have made you feel like a superstud in the sack.

EDWARD: Do I have to remind you that I am English? We do not have sex. We go to the races.

JUDY: And with her you could combine the two right in your own bedroom.

EDWARD: How dare you.

JUDY: Oh, come on, fast Eddie. You know she made you feel like you had Big Ben chiming in your pants.

EDWARD: All right, I admit it. She made me feel like a woman—no, I mean a queen—no a king. When she entered my boudoir, I—

JUDY: You whipped out the saddle.

EDWARD: You know, Judy, Wallis loved animals as I did. She surrounded herself with pedigree pug dogs.

JUDY: Yeah, well, next to them even she'd look like a fox.

EDWARD: I will not tolerate this badgering of my precious Duchess. She was impeccably groomed.

JUDY: Well, so was Flicka, but you don't see me slipping a wedding ring on his hoof.

EDWARD: That's your loss. You don't know what you're missing.

JUDY: So at least you admit it.

EDWARD: Yes, yes, I acquiesce. Why fight it? She was a true thoroughbred.

JUDY: She was the closest thing to Trigger in a skirt, right?

EDWARD: [sobbing happily] Yes, Trigger, yes.

JUDY: And every Sunday at tea you'd take her to Hyde Park and she'd giggle with delight as the neighborhood kids rode her for a quarter each.

EDWARD: No, no. A dollar. I did not sell her cheap.

King Henry VIII

JUDY: Your Highness, why where you such a gluttonous, wife-killing pig?

HENRY: I am an absolute monarch. Food is meant to be eaten, and wives are meant to be beheaded.

JUDY: Oh, that's catchy. You should put that on a coffee mug, you gelatinous glob of hippo cellulite.

HENRY: Thank you, I don't mind if I do. [Starts chomping on a barbecued mule's head.] Judy, you know I lead a very clean and healthy life.

JUDY: Right, Jack LaLanne. I suppose it's perfectly normal for your stomach to explode from syphilitic gas and pork rinds eight hours after you've been dead.

HENRY: Did that happen to me?

JUDY: Yes, but of course you don't remember because you were dead. You blew up on your funeral pyre at Hampton Wick Castle and the dogs had a feast.

HENRY: Gross me out, goddess. . . . Well, at least I went out with a bang.

JUDY: Yeah, and you were only thirty-eight years old when you croaked, but you looked at least fifty-eight. What's your secret?

HENRY: Just lucky, I guess. And of course I was loved by many wonderful women.

JUDY: Right, Rex Rotundo. They loved you under penalty of death. Then as soon as they surrendered to your obese organ, you chopped off their heads.

HENRY: Why does a woman need a head anyway?

JUDY: Nice attitude, Henry Dice Clay. While you're at it, why not chop off their arms and legs so all you have left are breasts and a love tunnel.

HENRY: Hey, why didn't I think of that?

JUDY: Because you were too busy stuffing your fat face with mutton, you merciless misogynist. Hey, stick your skull in here, pig. I'm turning you into human headcheese. [I shove his face into the bellows of my squeeze box and grind him into lunch meat while he kisses my petite feet.]

JUDY: So Henry, how does it feel to be the king with a puss made of headcheese?

HENRY: I feel purged, cleansed.

JUDY: Good, olive-loaf face. Now, who was your favorite wife?

HENRY: Anne Boleyn. She had three hooters.

JUDY: So you beheaded her.

HENRY: She could not bear me a son. I needed a male heir.

JUDY: What do you call Elizabeth I. Tell me she wasn't a guy in a gown.

HENRY: True . . . but this is all making me very hungry. I want food.

JUDY: How about a nice headcheese sandwich?

HENRY: Sounds great . . .

·IV·

INDOCTRINATION

INTO

JUDYISM

Purgatory Dating

Just try to tell me you subvirgins and slug puppies haven't done this. You're in a relationship with some oinklet that has degenerated from a few nights of blissful poking to frantic moments of stuffing each other into body bags. You're semi-dating the trog until something even slimier crawls along. You're not exactly burning in hell; you're just numb from trying to keep your once passionate sex bag from turning into a satellite dish for ESPN. But the very thing that attracted you to the little boy is the thing that repels you. In short, babies were meant to be born, not married, OK, you drooling eating machines in diapers?

What's even more depressing than dating a mechanically inclined infant who can't put the toilet seat down?

Dating in the dark. Remember when you had a really low self-image or you just felt kinda moody about some silly little complex that no one else would even notice? Most of the population wouldn't begin to notice that you were seven thousand pounds overweight, but just because you're self-conscious about squirting others with your blowhole, you spent most of your adult life in bed dreaming about jumping through hoops at Sea World.

Or it's prom night and you have a slight blemish, totally undetectable to the naked eye. When people laugh and call you volcano face, it's just to build up your sissy character. You resemble Mount Vesuvius in a tanktop. You don't want to be stared at, so you go out on the prowl after midnight. But the problem is that you never get a good look at your date because it's pitch-dark outside, and the only guys available at that hour are owls who deal drugs or vampires who bake bread. Or Richard Simmons advertising Deal-a-meal.

And isn't it curious that he never invites you to his place? He makes excuses like, "Oh, you wouldn't like my pad. The maid got sick, so it kinda stinks." Yeah, it stinks all right, because it's the trunk of his Pacer.

At first you think it's really cute that he's man enough to share his eating disorder with you. But then he doesn't even try to hide the fact that he's just using you for your shower. You think you'd get the hint. Night after night he rolls up to your door wrapped in swaddling clothes, crying, "Can you believe I still don't have hot water?"

OK, virginettes, leave the room. It's time for goddess-to-stud talk. Squid starters, why is it that you can't figure out that a nude blonde who lives in your jockstrap is not gonna sign a prenuptial agreement? My favorite are the millionaires on respirators who say, "Oh, she's so cute, and I know it's true love . . . she sits on my lap for hours." No kidding, gramps. She's looking for your wallet.

*T*he *S*ecret of *E*ternal *L*ove

As the supreme Love Goddess and Venus of Virility, so many pseudovirgins confess to me that they worry and wonder about when to submit to a stud puppet. *Never!* Except, of course, if you want to be in the movies or get a promotion; you must always make the fragile male feel that he has a rocket booster in his pants. Tell him that even NASA is in awe of his mammoth missile. Any anal-retentive pig in a three-piece suit will swallow that load, and you'll skyrocket straight to the top of the hog futures market.

But in your personal life, when you're on a one-to-one basis with a stud puppet, always keep your legs crossed.

Even if you marry him, Super Glue your thighs and never let the slug see you. He'll be crazy about you. Why? Because, you naive nymphets, absence makes the rod grow stronger. I mean it, make the pig fantasize, never ever let him *possess* you. In fact, the ideal would be to make him date a hologram of you while you're out pollinating other porkbellies.

I know some of you Mary Kay Pink Cadillac worshippers are plotzing now, but think about it. All the great love stories are based on some poor pining plankton who can't pounce on the petite princess of his dreams. Look at *Wuthering Heights.* Do you think for one minute that if Cathy surrendered to Heathcliff he would be half as crazy about her? No way. He was in love with his fantasy of that floozie. Even after Cathy marries some society squid that she doesn't love, Heathcliff pursues her and says, "Cathy, nothing can come between our love; not even you." What a great line. Women the world over dream about such passionate prose from some pumped-up parasite.

Cathy says, "Heathcliff, I'm married. Why did you come after me?"

He says, "Because you willed it."

Could you hemorrhage, heifers?

Heathcliff repeats, "I'm here because you willed it, Cathy." How could she not melt? I'm yelling, "Cathy, you fool, lay down already, loosen your lovesick loins." But Cathy is no fool, she knows that as a true romantic, giving into love would be the death of lust. So she spurns Heathcliff again and he is even more mental about possessing her.

Why can't we petite flowers in the real world find a passionate love puppy like Heathcliff? Because they do not exist. Neither do Romeos or Othellos. These guys can afford to be passionate about their Juliets and Desdemonas because they don't have to earn a living like every other mortal toad. Their passion for these unattainable princesses is their work. It consumes them, devours them, but their fire would be doused in an instant if these broads put out. In fact, it is only when Cathy and Juliet are dead that they can finally consummate their passion. Perfect. What does this tell us? That you can only live the perfect love when you are dead. Thanks, but I'd rather meet the pig of my dreams by turning on the VCR than by sticking a spear through my guts.

The Pig Club for Men

So many petite virginettes ask, "Oh Judy, why does my man turn into a pig when another man enters the room?" Your love thing may be as sweet as pecan pie and as submissive as a Play-Doh puppie when he needs food and lodging for his love log. But once the wild sex beast is satisfied, he has to reinforce his maleness by hooting, howling, and rolling with his piggy pals like a bunch of hardhats verbally humping a passing porkette.

My own brothers act like this. One on one, they are some of the most precious primates in captivity. For example, my brother Bosco 1 once said, "Judy, I saw you on 'Joan Rivers,' you were great." Then my brother Bosco 3 slithers into the room and they immediately get possessed by Hoss Cartwright and squeal, "Hey Judy, act like a girl and fix us some grub." Right, like I'm gonna get tied to the stove and fry hog grits for these goobers.

There must be an unwritten code that when two or more studs get together with a female present, they have to assert their extra Y chromosomes to make sure their testosterone is still intact. Let's face facts. It's kind of a minor tip-off that in the reproductive process all a stud puppet has to do is contribute his seed. Oh thanks, Jack in the Beanstalk. But we fertile femmes are the ones who have to power-bloat for nine months and give birth to a screaming mass of cells that will one day shoot us for the Mazda.

What ever happened to the kind of pig who rolled you in the mud and snatched your purse to play poker with the boys? Now all the pigs want is a commitment. It makes me barf. These whimpering Alan-Alda-family-focused-dead-men-do-eat-quiche hogs all whine, "It's the nineties, I'm a caring male." Yeah, you mean a male carrier.

Now all these baby-men either want a 1-900-Jessica Hahn slut whose entire body is donated by Du Pont or they want a multimedia bondage goddess like myself to discipline them. Like I have time to spank some sperm whale with a Visa card.

*M*ore *L*etters to the *G*oddess

Dear Judy,

My pet schnauzer, Sigmund, just croaked. Do you believe in doggie afterlife?

Sally Science

Yes I do. In fact, if you have a black standard poodle, it's your duty to shoot him. Then he can reach the next level of reincarnation: an A.M. disc jockey.

o   o   o

Dear Goddess of Love,

After ten years of marriage, my husband and I have

fallen into a romantic rut. Why can't our relationship be more like Romeo and Juliet's?

Abigail Angst

Because you're both still breathing.

o o o

Dear Judy, Queen of Candypants,
  I am a big fat fag who desires deep butt sex. Will you marry me and pay my medical bills?

Love,
Harry Hole

Count on it, Patient Zero. Become a congressional page and pack fudge for Fannie Mae.

o o o

Dear Judy, Earth Mother,
  I am an anti-nuke, anti-armpit-shaving feminist who wants to nurture. Should I take over the world or have a baby?

Rebecca Rugmunch

Do both. Date a sperm bank, and sit on a globe, and rotate.

o o o

Dear Judy,
  My brother Dworko and I were separated at birth and given to different parents. Twenty years later we married, not knowing we were brother and sister until eighteen of our thirty-two kids came out like cumquats. What should we do?

Signed,
Patricia Pube

Move to Indiana and become Vice-President of the United States.

o o o

Dear Judy,

I am a very attractive sixty-six-year-old lesbian librarian with a lisp and a clubfoot. Where can I find a man?

Gertrude Whine

Go to a golf course, Gertrude.

o　o　o

Dear Exalted One,

My mother says that you are not a living saint, and that I should not be a member of Judyism! In fact, she is having me deprogrammed by a Young Republican.

Dan Quayle

Your mom is just a big fat piece of space junk who is jealous because I have ESP and she has PMS. Just keep chanting my name and the Young Republican will freak out from your use of polysyllables.

o　o　o

Dear Judy, Saint of Svelteness,

I weight six thousand pounds and I'm so fat even Dick Gregory can't pry me out of my bathtub. Do you think Judyism can help me?

Rosanne Barrstool

Perhaps this poem may give you hope:

> If you're blah and fat
> And you know you're not too swift
> Just call me up collect
> And I'll send you a forklift.

o　o　o

Dear Judy,

Is it so wrong to shoot a moon at the president while he's addressing the House of Representatives?

Sincerely,
Mrs. Barbara Bush

Knock yourself out, Babs.

o   o   o

Dear Judy,

I am an incarcerated man. I am on death row just because I ax-murdered a couple of bag ladies on their way to bingo. But it wasn't my fault; I ate a Twinkie. Can I plead not guilty by reason of junk food?

Love, Bundtcake Manson

P.S. Will you marry me? I don't want to burn in hell.

Dear Bundtcake,

You really screwed up, pal. You can't just murder two or three people; it looks like you're not very good at what you do. You have to murder thirty people and you'll get your own game show. And if you murder three hundred, you'll get a miniseries starring Richard Chamberlain as you. Sure, I'll marry you. Dream on, Klingon.

o   o   o

Dear Judy,

I am a buxom blond aerobics instructor with a genius IQ, but no one respects me for my intelligence.

Signed,
Debbie Buttslammer

Dear Miss Buttslammer,

We all know that even Marie Curie could never have discovered radium if she didn't bench-press her keyster twelve hours a day to Michael Jackson tapes. So don't lose hope.

o   o   o

Dear Judy,

I am engaged to be married in June. I am a Christian, so my future wife and I will not have sex until after the children are dead. The problem is my fiancée has never seen me naked. Do you think I should tell her about the six-foot mime growing out of my buttocks?

Rectal Roberts

Just tell her it was a war injury you got in San Francisco.

o   o   o

Dear Judy,

I am a middle-aged glass blower who worships Satan. Can I have your panties?

Lucy Furr

Call Geraldo.

o   o   o

Dear Judy,

I am a big-time Broadway producer who tries to hide my success by living in the subway. Will you feed me?

George M. Conehead

No, toad, just keep passing out coupons in front of Taco Bell.

o   o   o

Dear Judy,

When is it OK to eat another person to stay alive?

Dick Clark

Whenever you're hungry, Piggly Wiggly.

o   o   o

Dear Blesser of Bunions,

Every night for the last twenty years, my husband has been sending me into the kitchen to make popcorn. Last week I found out he was getting me out of the way just so he could have sex with our son in the living room. The question is, will all the salt and butter be bad for his heart?

Signed,
Batterina Doormat

Dear Batterina,
    Just shut up and go on Oprah.

o   o   o

Dear Wise One,
    Last night my wife and fifteen daughters all got their periods at the same time. Needless to say, I was forced to go outside my home for sex. The problem is now my neighbors are suing me just because their poodle can't walk.

Sincerely,
David Duke

Elope with Batterina Doormat.

o   o   o

Dear Judy, Love of my Life,
    Last week I chopped off half my buttocks and sent it to you. Why didn't you respond?

Sincerely,
Prince Charles

Dear Prince,
    If you're gonna do something, do it all the way, not half-assed.

o   o   o

Dear So-called Goddess,
    If you are so famous, why don't you have an amusement park in the shape of your breasts?

Sincerely,
Conway Twitty and Jim Bakker

Dear Pigs,
    What do you think I am, an egotist?

*T*he
"I'm OK, You're a Fat Cow"
*W*eight *L*oss *P*lan

This is the Gospel for all bulbous bipeds who are begging to be me. Now listen: if you are a gargantuan glob of gourmet gonads, the only way I'll let you kiss my feet is if you stay in shape.

Let's assume you are a fat pig. (By definition, a fat pig is anyone who is not me.) So if you are the aforementioned porker, you can either a) beach yourself or b) hire me to eat your food and sit on top of your intergalactic girth until you explode. Or, if you want to flaunt your fatness, just go to the Chicago stockyards and hang from a meat hook until Sylvester Stallone pounds you into the pulp of a pig that you are.

Hire Judy to sit on your intergalactic girth.

FILOSOPHY OF FOOD

Remember, toad, food is meant to be not eaten but dis-played. Food is a tool that leads to friends and fame. You need food, not to stay healthy but to appear rich.

To appear rich, keep lots of food around . . . but never eat it. You must starve yourself so you'll look like one of Sally Struthers's Third World kids waiting for Uncle Sam to drop ten tons of farina on your head by helicopter.

Instead, just invite fat, festering friends over to feast. Which will be difficult, because you never see fat people eat. Offer them a celery stick and they say, "No thanks, I'm on a diet." Then you turn around and they've inhaled the fridge.

So pretend not to see the bisons balloon up on your barbecued butt steaks. While they're grazing, tell "60 Min-utes" that you and Jane Fonda are solving the world weight problem by sucking the fat out of obese people and turning them into shelters for the homeless.

So live by the three F's—Food, Fame, and Friends—and you won't be a fat, freeloading disco ferret.

To stay thin, never eat—but keep tons of food and invite fat friends to feast on it.

MIND CONTROL AND FOOD

How many times have you said to yourself, "Judy, Juudy." Yes, you thought you were me. How many times have you said, "Oh, Judy, I have such a taste for a hot fudge sundae . . . but I know it would be bad for me." So instead you got a complete blood transfusion.

But you still had a taste for a hot fudge sundae, and that craving crept into your romantic life. And you said, "Juudy, Juudy, I've always wanted to date a very handsome male model who's kind of mean, but I know he would be bad for me. So instead I'm dating a big fat pig with a nice personality, and I have to have a hot fudge sundae just to deal with it." So never deny yourself, donkey enticer.

Don't date a big fat pig with a nice personality or you'll have to have a hot fudge sundae just to deal with it.

In fact, once a week, you should pig out. That's right, little heifer, every Wednesday you must eat like you're going to the electric chair. Shovel in that pasta with both hands and feet, 'til they pull the switch and you become a crispy fritter.

Look, love leech, we all get cravings. So the next time you feel the need to inhale a Clydesdale, just go to the park instead, and watch a Hari Krishna get French-kissed by a jackhammer. It's less fattening.

If you're trying to knock off some beef, remember: always eat breakfast. Your first meal of the day is the most important. Why? Because if you don't down a bran muffin before you walk out the door and get hit by a truck, you'll be dead on an empty stomach. Toast half a buffalo on a bagel—but NEVER EVER USE BUTTER; cholesterol clog.

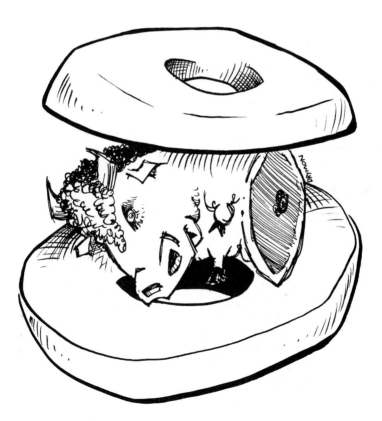

Judy's perfect breakfast: Toast half a buffalo on a bagel.

THE POWER OF CHOCOLATE

So good, I'm staying at this very fancy hotel, the Jimmy Swaggart Saddle-a-Slut Motor Inn, and they keep putting chocolate on my pillow, and it piles up because I forget about it. So one night, I fell asleep on a whole pillowful of chocolate, and it smears all over the petite flower face.

When the maid smashes in the door at 4 A.M. the next morning and screams, "Housekeepin'," she sees me and says, "Giiiiiiiiiirl, what happened to you?" I said, "Woman, I'm Othello, and you're Desdemona, so lay down and swallow this pillow."

And she never made my bed with chocolate again.

CHINESE RESTAURANTS ARE A NO-NO

Excuse me, Eggroll-Phile, but have you ever noticed (I promise never to use that hackneyed, observational Andy Rooney phrase again) that Chinese restaurants are a plot to overthrow America? I can prove it, wonton toad.

Only Americans go to Chinese restaurants, where we are waited on by three-pound geisha girls, carrying seven thousand pounds of Cantonese cuisine on each arm. They keep schlepping gargantuan platters of sweet-and-sour Rae Dong-Chong, but if this stuff is so great, why don't they eat it? They obviously don't or else they'd weigh more than a Karen Carpenter doll. But they keep serving it to us, and we gorge on it until the Census Bureau declares each of us a continent.

Chinese restaurants are a no-no.

Nick Tubolardi, my first ex-boyfriend.

OBSESSION WITH THINNESS

My ex-boyfriend Nick Tubolardi was a blimp. (OK, he wasn't really my boyfriend, he was more like this thing I sat on.) He'd drink milk right from the cow and then put it back in the refrigerator with his fat pig germs on it. So one night for his birthday, I wired his jaw shut, and before the earth could rotate around him, he lost 500 pounds.

So now he's down to a svelte 700 pounds and he becomes an airline hostess. That's right, all of a sudden he thinks he's hot hamhocks just 'cause he can fit his caboose into a pressurized cabin without the use of a shoehorn. I don't need that kind of threat to a relationship.

It was so wonderful when he just vegged out in my living room like a bulbously bloated beanbag chair. He matched my drapes and my friends had a place to park their useless carcasses. Now I have to go out and buy a couch. The fat pig. I mean it as a compliment.

FAT IS BEAUTIFUL

I want all disgustingly bloated swamp sows to know that I, the Petite Flower, think fat is beautiful. In fact, I can't stand these anorexic fashion sluts who eat five cakes and then stick their fists down their throats so they can fit into their Calvin Klein candypants. Then they whine, "Oh Judy, I eat and eat and I can never put on weight." Yeah well, just lay down and I'll drop the UN building on you. That oughtta pack on the pounds, Paulina.

Not like my roommate, Blowsanne. She's two-feet-one, 690 pounds, and a mime. One day she said, "Judy, I'm soooo fat, I can't get out of bed to make eggs."

So that night, while she was sound asleep, I inserted a Teflon plate in her lower lip. That way she could just fry and swallow.

I'm such a giver, I even got her a job modeling . . . with Manatee Fashions, an agency for full-figured sea cows. But she's so huge, she couldn't fit into human clothing. I mean it . . . she models houses. One day I went to one of her fashion shows and as she was bouncing down the aisle, the moderator announced, "And here's Blowsanne, showing a lovely Dutch colonial."

My roommate, Blowsanne, modeling a Dutch Colonial.

WHY WE OVEREAT

The reason we so often eat like Romans is because food is everywhere . . . we no longer have to hunt for it like our ancestors did. And I love to hunt, 'cause I look divine in safety orange.

My favorite part of hunting is when after you shoot the deer, you smear its blood all over your face to prove you're not afraid of a dead defenseless animal. It makes me feel like a woman!

We'd all be a lot healthier if we had to forage for our Fritos, instead of driving to the Piggly Wiggly. So, the next time you need food, club a mushroom and eat it with your bare hands. You will develop your deltoids while devouring a fungus.

BEFORE WE WERE YUPPIES, WE WERE FOOD

Let's go back in time. Remember when we were all cream-of-chromosome soup? Slimy little amoebas (now known as used car salesmen) swimming around in paramecium pants? Then we evolved into fish. That is why you must never eat seafood: it is a mortal sin to consume your ancestors. Deal with it, Catholics.

To this day I cannot go fishing. Every time I look at a wide-mouthed bass I see Sandra Bernhard. Besides, it's not fair to the little fishies, cuz they don't have arms to fight off my bullets.

Secret Diets
of the Goddess

The Emergency Room Diet

Go to the emergency room of any hospital. (I like St. Joseph's 'cause they hand you a baby aspirin after you've been guillotined.) Then have every toad in the place show you his colostomy bag while you try to wolf down a Whopper.

The Great Dictator Diet

Remember, food is power. If you can't have power, you crave food. So whenever you get the irresistible urge to appoint yourself dictator of your country and steal billions from the treasury, just preheat the oven to 500°, then bake yourself into a Pol Pot Pie.

If you're a woman, make yourself into an Imelda Marcos omelette. Simply deep-fry your frozen hog embryo eggs, then garnish with six hundred pairs of pumps.

The Boa Constrictor Diet

Lock yourself in a cage and don't eat for three years. Then swallow a donkey whole (to get the full nutrient value).

The Break Up with Your Boyfriend Diet

1. Have the pig leave you for some fetus in candypants after you've put him through law school.
2. Look at all his pictures while sitting in a tub of ice cubes and sniffing his stanky sweatsocks, soaked in rotten egg yolks.
3. Smear the egg white all over your face.
4. Join the mime workshop at your local Moose lodge.

*J*udyism *D*iets from *A*round the *W*orld

(For All You Globes)

Diet of Rome

1. Lie down, clown.
2. Have a nun or a gangster (like there's a difference) shove pasta into your puss until you look like the Coliseum.

SERVES ONE ITALIAN FETUS

Diet of Mexico

1. Borrow ten billion dollars from the Bank of America (or Neil Bush).
2. Use the money to build a giant gold statue of the Virgin Mary.
3. Pray to it for food.

SERVES ZERO

New York City Diet

Sit on a toilet for eight hours until an alligator that you purchased in Miami for your spoiled brat pops up from the sewer and bites off your bulbous buns.

SERVES ONE ALLIGATOR

Diet de France

1. Spend six years' income on a Dior original while not bathing for half a century.
2. Take a shovel and plunge it into your neighbor's swamp.
3. Snort anything that doesn't look like Jerry Lewis.

SERVES SIX PRETENTIOUS WOMANIZERS

The Soviet Drinking Woman's Diet

1. Attach a tractor to your rear end. (Not too redundant.)
2. Wait in line ten hours to suck the wine stain out of your premier's head.

SERVES THREE DISSIDENT DAMSELS

The German Diet

1. Preheat the oven to 6000° (take the non-Aryan out first, pig).
2. Have everyone in your village not change their Lied-erhosen for sixty years until you all mistake each other for Liverwurst. (Don't stink too much or you'll have to go to France.)

SERVES YOU RIGHT

The Bohemian Diet

Eat only at other people's houses.

SERVE YOURSELF

The Diet of India

Once and for all let's clear up the myth about Gandhi. The guy was bulimic. No, I mean it. Plus his idea of a soft drink makes me kinda queasy. He's too cheap to buy lemonade so he approximates it with his own fluids. Really appetizing, diaper dude.

When I first met Gandhi, he was an upper-middle-class lawyer in an H & R Block suit. I said, "Look, squid. You're supposed to save people's souls, not do their taxes. Take that calculator out of your crotch and put on some Pampers." Once again the fashion-plate saint molds another religious leader.

I said, "Gandhi, don't you ever eat?"

He said, "Sure, but did you ever notice that when you're just a little bit hungry because you haven't eaten in a decade and you munch a tiny potato chip, the next thing you know you're inhaling Idaho to satisfy your dormant fat-pig cells? Then your stomach expands to the size of a small dictatorship and you have to swallow whole continents just to be satisfied. And all this just because you were a baby petite bit hungry. But if you ignore your infantile hunger pangs, they go away and your pig stomach shrinks. Then finally you start to resemble the ideal: a Giacometti sculpture. *(For all you brain-dead trolls who never leave the sports bar to go to the museum, this is a Giacometti):*

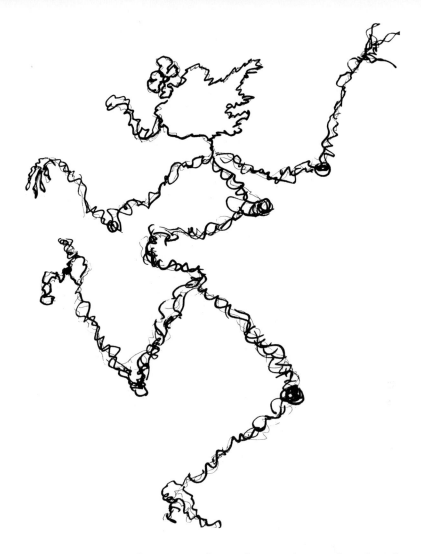

Now you're thin enough to share a brown-bag lunch with Helen Boney Brown, the editor of *Cosmo*, who looks like Skeletor in a dress. You see, it's so simple: Stop eating. Eating is for weaklings. Put a muzzle on your mouth and call up Dick Gregory to smack out your fat cells, then you'll be a petite saint. And as an extra bonus, with that bear trap on your puss, you can be hired as a guest villain in the next James Bond flick. So lose the flab, and gain a film career.

It could happen.

The Red China Diet

1. Sit in a circle with a billion other people from the same gene pool.
2. Eat rice and multiply until your government lets you watch TV.

OVER ONE BILLION SERVED

Diet of England

With all due respect to our motherland, the English think we Americans are retarded just because we use deodorant. Well, excuse us, your royal colonial vampireness, but at least we don't live on congealed pig's blood and marry our own grandmothers. OK, except maybe in Alabama. Goooood.

I'm sorry, but why is it that only in England every six-year-old boy is a shepherd who falls hopelessly in love with his 112-year-old grandmother as she bends over to pick up her teeth? If you don't believe me just read the *National Enquirer*, OK, trogs?

Nice, in England they tax their own bowel movements and give the money to the Queen. They don't find it a bit incongruous that they're all coalminers on strike living in a feces hut, and the Queen has 70 billion dollars in bus change alone.

They say, "But Judy, we love the Queen. She gives us someone to look up to." Yeah, well so does an amoeba. They retort, "The Queen is worth every penny because each June fourteenth she rides backward on a horse and waves."

I ask you, is it any wonder we left to discover America and toilet paper?

English Weight Loss Breakfast

---

1. Take five vats of triple-bleached white flour.
2. Deep-fry in twelve barrels of nineteenth-century locomotive oil until tasteless.
3. Cover with congealed pig's blood.
4. Marry your grandma.

SERVES ONE ENGLISH BOY

Two Special Love Slave Recipes

Sexist Pigs in a Blanket

Roll your IBM brood sow boss in a raw dough, then pinch his corporate buns with a cattle prod until he serves you coffee.

Mass Murderer Mousse

Mass murderers have no creative outlet, so they become walking Veg-O-Matics. If Hitler could have become the great artist he always wanted to be, he might have used his puny male punching bag to paint a Polish landscape instead of invading it.

To make mass murderer mousse, you will need three mass murderers (like Gacy, Bundy, and Hitler):

1. Throw them into a blender.
2. Have the relatives of their victims press "puree."
3. Pour into petite flower bowls.
4. Garnish with a tank.

SERVES SIX MILLION

Don't Exercise . . . Goddessize!

The following exercises are not for sissified slime tarts,
so slap on the sweatpants and buckle up,
love squid!

The Cardiovascular Workout

The best way to build up your heart rate is not to jog, no.
Just stand nude—that's right, completely raw—in the middle of the ghetto wearing only a hundred gold chains. As
soon as you see those crack kings, your pulse will slam-
dance.

The Couples Workout

Let's say you and your mate are a couple of globes. Sit on the floor. (As if you can do anything else.) With your hooves touching, grunt until you sweat like sun-drenched sows. Press paws facing each other and hold. (Make sure you're both sitting on a hot plate to make it burn.)

Note: This exercise should be done with at least sixty skinny people laughing at you, to build up your adrenaline.

The Pet Rock Workout

Let's say you are an octogenarian fossil who smokes cigars like George Burns at a Ubangi bar mitzvah. Simply puff on a White Owl while speed-walking through a cancer ward, then wait for the terminal patients to club you with their catheters until you become a pet rock and can only be used as a doorstop.

They will get exercise and you will finally have a purpose.

The Jewish Princess Workout

Stay in bed and complain.

The Like a Virgin Workout

Stick your head in a vat of Clorox. Hold. Then parade around like a giant professional breast until some lesbo lip with feet vacuums your rug.

The Shirley MacLaine Workout

1. Pass a crystal the size of Venus through your vag.
2. Pay some senile guru eight thousand bucks to tell you that you used to be Cleopatra's toe jam in a past life.

Weeping Widow Workout

If you are in your mid-trillions and used to baby-sit for Moses:

1. Go into the lobby of your nursing home.
2. Sit in a semicircle with at least nineteen other fossil women.
3. Whine about how each of your husbands just died of lung cancer as you all chain-suck Salems.

The Linda Evans Cheekbone Workout

1. Empty your mind of all thoughts (first making sure that your talent is hidden).
2. Purse your lips together. Hold.
3. Touch your cheekbones to the ceiling. Hold.
4. Chant continuously, "I would gladly give up five million dollars a year if I could just be a wife and mother."
5. Date millionaire after millionaire, breaking up with each one as soon as he builds you a mansion.
6. Give every mansion to some six-thousand-year-old channeler named Ramtha.

The Prime-Time Cow Workout

Gain 600 pounds and graze until you get your own shitcom. Then leave your husband and kids for some thug who is blind enough to poke you so he can sell the story to *Better Homes & Blimps*.

More Letters to the Goddess

Dear Judy, Love Goddess Supreme,
   I am your biggest fan and I would walk a mile in
Cher's soiled panties to worship you.

Respectfully,
Sonny

Dear Sonny,
   Get real, Captain Tenille. You'd walk a mile in Cher's
soiled panties, *period.*

o   o   o

Dearest Judy,

   In your infallible opinion, which comics have the longest careers?

Sincerely,
Earl Butts

Dear Mr. Butts,

   The ones who smoke cigars and/or do Jell-O Pudding commercials.

o   o   o

Dear Judy,

   My boyfriend, whom I love very much, has left me for another woman. What should I do?

Sadly,
Yeasty McCrevis

You should be patriotic. Which means, as a true American, if you cannot eat or own something, it is your duty to destroy it.

o   o   o

Dear Judy,

   Is there sexism in the world of comedy?

Your Loving Libber,
Hugh Hefner

Dear Hef,

   Does Rose Kennedy own a black dress? You bet your air-brushed breasts there is. I had to grow a twelve-foot ego and stuff it in my pants just to get this far. That's why I'm known as Judy "The Wad" Tenuta.

o   o   o

Dear Judy,

   I am very angry that you have not returned my solid gold "walk on me" spiked heels.

Irately Yours,
Imelda Marcos

Dear Imelda,
Now you know how all your countrymen feel. By the way, I lent the solid gold submission pumps to Nancy Reagan. Just try to get them back from her, squidlet.

o   o   o

Dear Judy,
How can a mother tell if a new baby-sitter is going to rip the house apart or batter the kids?

Petula Poundoff

It's kind of a hint that you made a poor choice if the guy asks to be paid upfront in bananas.

o   o   o

Dear Judy,
I worship the ground you walk on even though I am just a giant bedpan with feet. Please play a polka on my face and then spank me with a giant bratwurst.

Wait in line, Ted Kennedy.

o   o   o

Dear Judy,
How can you tell when you first meet a guy whether he has the potential to become violent or not?

Inquisitive in Ipsalanti

Dear Inquisitive,
It's kind of a minor tip-off that your Romeo may be a tad temperamental if his name is Muammar and he is sitting on a rooftop with a rifle.

o   o   o

Dear Judy,
What do you think of Elizabeth II, Queen of England?

Sir Winston Stuffsnout IV

She's just like Disneyland, except you're not allowed to ride her. Unless you have a quarter.

o   o   o

Dear Judy,

I am a fifty-six-year-old Eagle Scout who lives in the woods with my mother. One day I got kinda hungry so I stuck her on a spit and barbecued her. Now she won't even talk to me. I'm scared.

Jeffrey Dahmer

You heartless thug. Did you even bother to baste her? No. You deserve to be Smokey the Bear's butt boy.

o   o   o

Dear Judy,

How do you like your men?

Renee Richards

Dear Renee,

I like my men the way I like my subway trains. Hot, packed, and unloading every three minutes.

Fashion Tips
from the Goddess

The ideal is for everyone, including myself, to be me. To want to be anyone else, of course, would be blasphemy—not only because I am the supreme goddess of Judyism, but also because I am the fashion-plate saint and queen of candypants. Mere mortals mutilate one another to collect my garbage, just to don some of my used dominatrix duds. As a petite flower, I always wear an overgrown Three Mile Island water lily in my hair, a chain of discipline from my eighth-grade nun, a silver-studded belt from Elvis, and bondage boots from Jed Clampett.

But let's say I couldn't be me, because I had to go undercover to work miracles. Then of course I would settle

Babs Bush with the fashion sense of Yasir Arafat.

for being Babs Bush (with the fashion sense of Yasir Arafat).
Imagine walking around like a human sofabed with a towel
on your head—what a magnificent distraction from death.

PSEUDO-VIRGIN FASHIONS FOR
HUSBAND HUNTING
(Ladies Only)
(I Mean Real *Ladies, Barry Manilow)*

Always act like a petite flower, but at the same time, let everyone know you'll mate with the first Shriner in a Saab. Let's face it, slutette, if you and your sisters had your way, you would all be big fat nudists. Like I have time to be visually electrocuted by your flopping flesh. No, I take that back; all you virginettes know that if there weren't studsicles to lick, you'd all be pigs in parkas. Admit it, you dress to be bounced on by belligerent bipeds with BMWs.

My favorite fashion floozies are these bimbettes who say "Judy, we're going love-hog hunting" and it's the dead of winter, and they're in see-through tops and spray-on jeans. Right, like some slug is gonna stick it in at forty below. Count on it, igloo ass.

Speaking of panties, let's pass the hat and buy some for Cher. I guess there's not enough pain involved in putting on bikini briefs, so it's better to have some drunken Bluto tattoo them onto your buttocks—perfect for the PTA, Cher. I'm sure Elijah Blue-Baby must be proud. Especially since he gets to bang the drums quickly while you boff a battleship, the USS *Slut*.

Let me tell you the classic tale of a taker. One night I was recruiting love slaves at the Palladium in New York City. Standing at the bar, just begging to be recognized, was Cher. I said, "How's it hanging, Sonny? Oh, is that you, Cher? I didn't recognize you with that mask on." And she never even offered me her Beverly Hills mansion or even her workout wig. Cher, you do not know the meaning of the word "share," your name should be take, not Cher. But I digress. (It's OK—I am the Duchess of Digression.)

Cher on the battleship, USS Slutcicle.

While husband hunting, always make sure you wear real subtle makeup, like Bette Davis in *Whatever Happened to Baby Jane?* Just trust me, petite hoggette.

After you do land a love hunk, when in doubt about how to make him submit, just be nude. I mean it, pseudo-virgin. Wear nothing but an accordion and yell, "Hey hog, where's my sex?" Subtlety is sacred.

When husband hunting, always be subtle.

If you really want to win a slime slug's heart, dress like his mother, with blue hair and a broom. Then bake him a big fat meat loaf, take him to a motel, and stab him in the shower.

FASHION NO-NOS

It's really attractive when a Mary Kay–wannabe mother with thirty kids hanging off her miniskirt is walking through the San Diego Zoo in twelve-inch pumps, causing her back porch to be arched like the space shuttle *Challenger* as she struts past the small primate house. Then she wonders why Boris the burly baboon bags her from behind. Perfect posture for rear entry, Sally Ride-a-Rump.

While zoo walking with your kids, never wear a micromini and ten-inch "pounce me" pumps or you'll arouse the apes.

(Speaking of simians, Epilady is of the devil. If you want to be a feminist fatale, grow hairy alf legs, wear a lumberjack shirt, and squeal like a pig.)

Another absolute fashion no-no is the beeper/business card coordinated combo. It's always at the most solemn moment of my Judyism gospel that some bozo's beeper goes off in his pants and he yells, "I'm needed at the hospital for a transplant." Right, dork, did they get some duck to donate a brain?

Then, as he's running out, he hands me a business card. Why aren't these things made out of toilet paper, so at least they'd serve a purpose?

Once even a coalminer handed me a business card and said, "Call me." Right, ape, I'll call you . . . when I need a lamp on my forehead.

THE FASHION CRAZE OF THE NINETIES

For the Super Fem:

Whether you want to get your beautician license, sponge off some used car salesman, or crack your gum like a black woman, you must take off your Refrigerator Perry shoulder pads and stick them under your stanky pits. That's right, super fem: Underarm shields will be the rage in the nineties.

For the Hot Hunk:

If you want to score like a super slug (although not with me, pretty Willy), make sure you wear elastic sock garters outside your pants—a major league turn-on.

Fashion craze of the nineties: underarm shields and sock garters.

FOR MEN ONLY

❦

Stud Puppet Make-over

Nothing is more of a turn-on than a beefy burrito with a beer gut blobbing around in boxer shorts, constantly clearing his throat. Yeah, I'll be spreading for that. Now listen up, love slug: If you want to be a Judy zombie, you must submit to a total stud puppet make-over. Simply:

Before   *During*

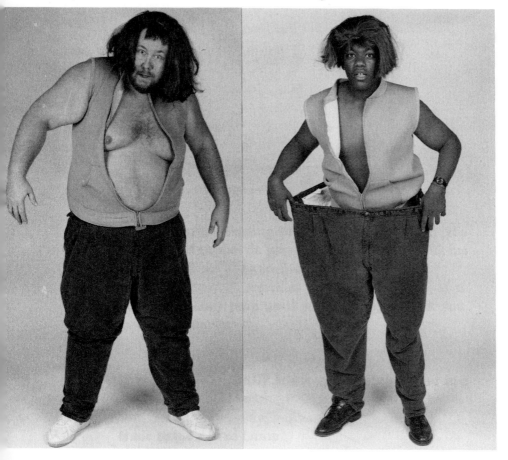

1. Hike your boxer shorts up to your jogging bra.
2. Put a Dr. Ruth safe sex cap on your skull.
3. Kneel down and beg to swallow my used goddess gum.

After

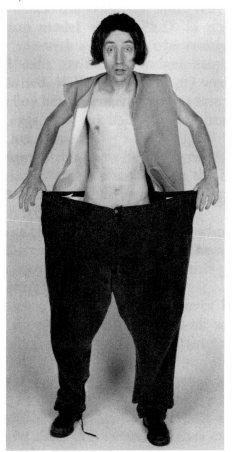

Giving of the Goddess Gum.

All stud puppets live to be furniture for the goddess.

If all men would dress like women, there would be no wars.

How to Prevent Wars

It's so simple. We would have no more wars if men would dress like women. Think about it. How could the enemy shoot at a front line of sex slugs in goldfish pumps and hotpants? They'd be too busy laughing.

HOW TO BE A FASHION FOX IN THE CITY OF YOUR CHOICE

How to be a fashion fox in Chicago.

Chicago

In Chicago, the hog butcher for the world, just drape a big fat side of beef on your bod and let starving subway mimes munch on you.

A New York City fashion fox.

New York City

If you're in New York City at an Andy Warhol punk feminist convention, dump yourself into a black bodybag, then bind your petite waist with Bigfoot's bike chain.

Be a fashion fox in Paris.

Paris

If you want a Paris original without the hefty price tag, do as the French do. Let your pits grow out, become a stranger to soap, and wear tons and tons of pink taffeta to distract people from your stench. Then have Catherine Deneuve hose you down with Chanel No. 5.

*W*here *N*ot to *M*ate

AT THE AIRPORT

Could someone just tell me: Are there invisible beds at the airport? Have you ever once seen a mattress at the gate with a sign that says, ROLL YOUR HOG HERE? *No!* Layaway plans are not allowed at departure gates. If I see one more troll vertically copulate with some pig who just got off a plane, I am personally allowed to blowtorch them into oblivion.

So many of you mortal mammals can't wait to spawn, but there's a time and place for mounting your love slug and this is *not* one of them. Get it, gal pals? It's just so queer. Like you can't wait five minutes to get into the back-seat of your Pinto Blow-Abouts to start a whole new recessive gene pool. And it's always these trogs—who look like

Never mate at the airport gate or the goddess may be forced to blowtorch you.

Junior Sample's back porch—who are the first to breed right on a nuclear waste dump . . . and then they wonder why they give birth to a Foot.

IN THE MIDDLE OF A FOOTBALL FIELD

What's the major malfunction of all these tight ends piling on top of each other, having a group orgy every five minutes? Don't they have a game to play? Oh, excuse me, you beefy burritos of manhood. Like you can't wait until half-time to pounce on your steroid-infested teammates.

If you'd stop wearing those skin-tight candypants and sex-machine shoulder pads, maybe you could concentrate on the game instead of one another's hot cross buns. From now on, all football players must wear the uniform of an eighth-grade Catholic girl: pleated skirt, combat boots, and gridiron braces. It worked for me, toads.

IN THE PARK

As a rule, it's really stupid to mate in the park with a Cub Scout troop, even if you are an archbishop. We all know that Catholic clergymen are fashion foxes in their Halloween costumes and Mr. Wizard Hats. They all look like walking MX missiles, ready for takeoff. Is it any wonder that the cubsicles turn Protestant? Nice.

MATING ADVICE: FOR SUPER FEMS ONLY
(I'm Warning You, Barry)

Don't ever mate with some pig just because you love him. If you have to sink that low, why not mount your parents? You love them, don't you? Well, see my point, squids?

Oh, I guess you're right; it's really smart to surrender your total being to some sponge that's gonna use you for a kitty litter box whenever he needs to empty his hot throbbing punching bags on the way to a Bulls game. From now on, don't even talk to these pigs unless they are willing to be my parents. You heard me, slutsicle: They must buy me gum, forever.

That is the true test of their love for you—what they are willing to do for me, Judy the petite flower, goddess of love. Bury this queer Cinderella story that some inbred toad with elephant ears is gonna shove a shoe on your foot and stuff you into a castle. Count on it, Leona Helmsley-head.

IN CHURCH

I'll never forget the time Wild Bill Coty, Archbishop of the Ground Round, came to our school and was so obese he couldn't fit through the church door, so all the altar boys were ordered to kneel down and feed him Oreo cookies until he exploded. Then, since he couldn't score with the boys, he bought a house for some middle-aged candy heiress using church funds. What's the point, you say? If he were allowed to get married, or at least date nuns, then maybe he wouldn't have to gain six tons and prey on prepubescent cub puppets.

AT A DAY-CARE CENTER

So many adult trogs want to prove that they're real good with toddlers. So they become teachers at day-care centers. They're not satisfied to check the kids for head lice. *No.* They make the tots get horizontal and play with clay by unzipping Mr. Pedophile's pants. But the kids can't find Gumbie cuz they forgot their 3D glasses. *But they didn't forget their video cameras* to record the valuable learning experience for the jury, who then sends the well-meaning pervert to prison where he will be forced to become a sexual bike rack for some toothless thug named Guido. I hope you kids are satisfied. Deliberately flaunting your two-year-old toddler tartness while sucking your thumbs on a rug. If that's not a turn-on, what is?

A DATING DON'T

No matter where you are, never deep kiss any troll who weighs under sixty pounds, even if he's dressed like me.

*W*here to *M*ate

AT A POLITICAL CONVENTION

Let's say you're an obscure political candidate running for ovular office. Even though you may be governor of the nation's largest chemical-waste dump, most Americans don't know who you are. So, to prove you are a people person, put on your best boxer shorts, fill your plastic pool with Bill Cosby Jell-O, and roll around with some brainless bimbo begging for a Playboy spread. Then accuse your political adversary of being a Nazi florist who burns flags. Now make sure a television crew is present, or at least invite Robin Leach with a megaphone. THE PEOPLE WANT A PRESIDENT WITH A PARTY PUD.

IN AN ELEVATOR

Let's say you and your mate have been legally bound since Zsa Zsa Gabor broke her cherry. Needless to say, your marriage needs a major jump start. So you and your fossil love pig should go to the nearest Saks Fifth Avenue elevator (it won't work at K mart, cuz they don't have elevators, OK, slugs?). Now, throw your walkers down and start humping away like Catholics at a Playboy Bunny bingo game. If you think your passion will last more than a New York minute, which is impossible since New York only has three-day blackouts, make the tallest toad press the emergency stop button until you reach Nirvana.

Still More
Letters to the Goddess

Dear Judy, Love Goddess Supreme,
  Because of you, our children have stopped taking drugs. Now they sell them. Please continue to bless us.
Love and Hair,
The Cowsills

Dear Cowsills,
  A family that snorts together, stays together.

o   o   o

Dear Judy,
  Who cuts your hair?

Wondering and Ready,
Jose Eber

Dear Jose,
  Babs Bush. And in return I trim hers.

o   o   o

Dear Yankee Bitch,
  If you had just one year left to live, how would you spend it?

Love,
Senator Jesse Helms

Dear Jesse,
  Teaching you the alphabet.

o   o   o

Dear Judy,
  Tenuta is such a funny sounding name. What does it mean?

Signed,
Engelbert Humperdink

Dear Engelbert,
  I can almost keep a straight face while saying your name. "Tenuta" is Swahili for "throbbing, impenetrable virgin."

o   o   o

Dear Love Goddess,
  Which part of your body are you most proud of? Do you pump up?

Sincerely,
Arnold Schwarzenegger

Dear Schwartz,
  Like you, I am most proud of my massive mamms. I

want to breast-feed Beirut. And I always pump before I hump.

o   o   o

Dear Judy,
    Which part of your body would you be most willing to part with?

Saddam Hussein

Dear Saddam,
    Are you guys that hard up for soup bones?

o   o   o

Dear Judy,
    When you started doing comedy clubs, how did everyone know you were a goddess?

Your Uncle,
Zeus

Dear Uncle Zeus,
    It was January 1978 at the Comedy Crack Hut in Chicago. There were seven people in the audience and fifty beginning comics waiting to tickle their funny bones. The club owner was at the mike introducing me and suddenly this huge rat ran across the stage. The owner whipped out a .357 Magnum, shot it, and said, "Ladies and gentlemen, please welcome Judy Tenuta." I knew I must be a goddess; already men were sacrificing small animals at my feet.

o   o   o

Dear Love Goddess,
    Who would you most want to be stranded with on a desert island?

Love,
Robinson Crusoe

Dear Robinson,
    I'd take Mr. Evian, squid.

o   o   o

Dear Judy,
    What ever happened to Baby Jane?

Curiously Yours,
Joan Crawford

Dear Joan,
    Like you don't already know she's on a wire hanger in your closet, Mommy Dearest.

       ○   ○   ○

To Our Lady of Laughter,
    Why do you like dogs better than cats?

Every Hack Comic in the World

Right, hacks, as if you guys don't sit in the kitty litter box for ninety-eight hours waiting for Felix to poop out your next punch line.

       ○   ○   ○

Dear Judy,
    I would floss with Bea Arthur's G-string just to be your sex slug.

Love,
Betty White

Dear Betty,
    Thanks for your unbridled enthusiasm, but for future reference, Bea Arthur wears a jock strap.

*A*re *Y*ou a *B*oy or *A*re *Y*ou a *G*irl?

I was in Irvine, California, and at the end of my love goddess show I rode some unsuspecting male troll into bondage. This time, however, as I was riding this blond crewcut yuppie, my hand was on his back and I felt a bra strap. Then it hit me: This is a woman dressed as a man. So I yelled, "I'm riding a dyke and she's in ecstasy. I thought it was a guy, but it's a broad who's creaming. Next time, I'll have to do a crotch check."

Not that it should matter whether you are a man or a woman, or a little of both, but if you are one of these sexually ambiguous types, don't sit smack-dab in front of me while I'm preaching the gospel accordion to Judy in a comedy club. Or, if you insist on sitting in the demilitarized zone and flaunting your undefinable sexuality, don't get your butt floss in an uproar when I ask, "Excuse me, are you a guy or a girl?" Especially if you're wearing a three-piece suit, earrings, and a mustache, with matching clod-hoppers and a purse. You obviously can't make up your androgynous mind, so I'll make it up for you. You are not a man or a woman, you are a *unitard*.

Isn't that great, you guys finally have a name: *uni-tards*. Now, thanks to the goddess you borderline women in lumberjack shirts and you chubby guys with baby faces and breasts have an identity: unitards. To be a full-fledged unitard, you should chant your mantra: "Sinead O'Connor, shave me," "Sinead O'Connor, shave me," paint a red *U* on your forehead, and whether you're a guy or a girl unitard, please wear a bra.

Lastly, I don't want the newly formed National Association of Unitards to protest my shows. I love unitards, I just need to know who you are. Better yet, please protest my shows, Sinead says I need the publicity. Thanks.

The Food Chain and Other Sponges

It's no secret that I am the lifeblood of the universe. I feed countless mouths, fill unlimited stomachs, and fatten in-numerable wallets just by my existence. In other words I am the top of the food chain and everyone else is dependent upon me for survival. In layman's terms, I keep a lot of sponges moist.

The biggest sponges—and I really have to let this out right here—are the hack jobs who try to pass themselves off as journalists and even that lowest of all life forms—the critic.

Not that I'm singling anyone out, but Siskel and Ebert should just anounce their engagement. They're like a couple of old maids on a date. They play hard to get with each other, but you know they can't wait to share Taster's Choice at the Y.

People magazine critics are the worst. In fact, if they give you an F as a grade it's a compliment, because their idea of an A is "Doogie Houser" or some hackneyed story about a prostitute who has found Jesus or some fat grazing sea cow with a tattooed ass and a series.

If these frustrated closet Lois Lanes with typewriters would just admit that they want to pop every prepubescent pup in sight, then maybe they could do something worthwhile with their lives, like serve me. But instead they have to hide their lust for boy toys and channel into hate for anything with a purpose.

(Of course, none of this is applicable if the critic is intelligent enough to totally adore me and hate everyone else.)

Wait, I just thought of something even lower on the food chain than the critic: ex-boyfriends who live in their Pacers and use you for your shower. These slugs are not even worthy of being hunted for food. *No.* They must die and be recycled as decayed fungus. And then they'll be ready to date a critic.

To illustrate how everyone is dependent on me for their survival, I now present the "Judy Food Chain":

The Judy food chain.

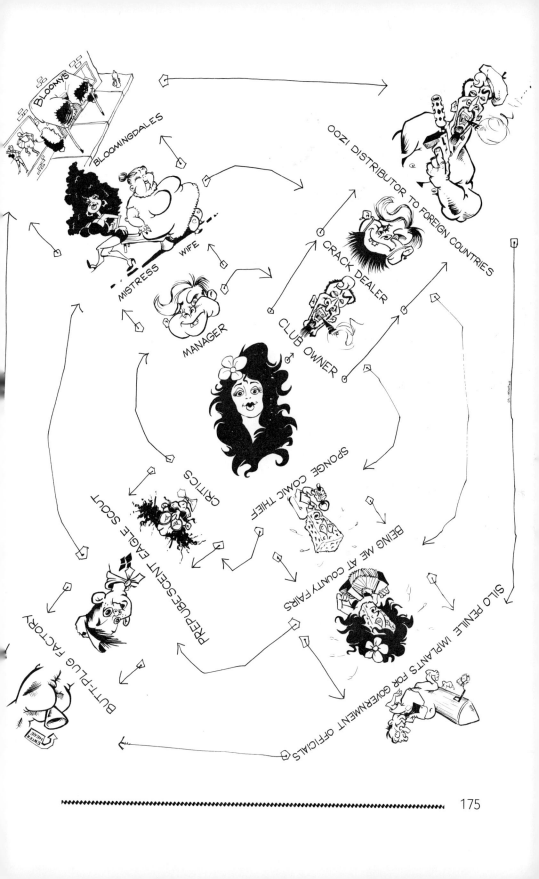

Pet Peeves
of the Goddess

The following are major mortal sins
against Judyism:

1. Trogs who compare the goddess to low-life swine by saying, "Hey Judy, you remind me of this Pig McMuffin who weighs three hundred pounds and grazes. You should watch her." Right, plankton. These same toads would meet God and say, "You remind me of George Burns. You should see him; you might learn something."

2. These squids who invite me to their homes for dinner, but instead of giving me food they say, "Hey Judy, come upstairs and look at our kids." Like I have time to see how their chromosomes mutated.

3. OK, so now I'm entering their new mansion. I'm at the front door and they say, "Hope you don't mind pets," as Sinbad the bed-wetting ape sweeps down on my skull and puts me in a headlock. Meanwhile, they've spent six million dollars for a palace that they fill with nine hundred cats so it can smell like a sewer in Saigon. Perfect.

4. A President who says, "I want a kinder, gentler nation," and who is a member of the National Rifle Association. Listen, Bushman, the right to bare arms means the right to wear sleeveless gowns.

5. When I go into a museum and touch an exhibit, but it's actually the security guard. She says, "Don't touch me."

I say, "I'm so sorry, I thought you were the first age of man."

She says, "No, I'm the security guard."

So I ask, "Can you please tell me where the petite flower, giver goddess ladies' room is?"

She yells, "Look for it yourself."

So I say, "Well, I was going by my sense of smell, but it led me to you."

6. Nine octogenarian fossils in graduation gowns who rule that they have control over women's bodies when they do not even have control over their own.

7. Men who say, "A woman is at her most beautiful when she's pregnant." But how come you go into the Bear's locker room and you never see a poster of some nude babe in her third trimester?

8. When I'm in England and I want to watch TV and the only choices are a twelve-hour special on the history of thread or the coronation of Baron Von Buttplug (or Prince Port-a-Potty or Prince Pinocchio Pants).

9. Fake fans who see a group of Judy zombies worshipping me and they decide to join in. Like once, this stain with feet says, "Judy, you're so great. I really admire your great courage and talent." And just as I'm giving her my autograph she says, "So what do you do? Are you a singer or what?"

10. A boorish eggplant who slobbers all over me and says, "Hey Judy, next time you're on TV mention my name." Right, like I'm gonna bring the show to a screeching halt in front of three million people, to say, "Hi, Trump."

11. These slug puppets who break up with you and then date some clone who looks just like you except she's donated her brain to shopping.

12. When I'm in line at the Stop & Rob at the fifty-items-or-less-aisle, and behind me is Tammy Faye Bakker, crying, "Hey Judy, let me get ahead of you ... my ice cream is melting." Yeah, well, take it out of your tube top.

Waiting in line at the airport ticket counter behind a fossil with a handbag.

13. When I'm at the airline ticket counter and I have a choice: To get in line behind two hundred trogs who are checking ten pairs of skis each, or stand behind an old bag with a purse. So of course I choose the old bag. Three hours pass and all the skiers have flown to Switzerland and back and this pet rock is playing Win, Lose or Draw with the ticket agent. I say, "Excuse me, Whistler's mother, could you please get a megaphone and describe every gallstone you and your poodle have had since Moses broke the tablets? That way, by the time I get my ticket I can collect my pension and make the trolls behind me wait 'til Christ returns to board a Mattel plane."

Later that century, still waiting behind the fossil.

14. When you're forced to be nice to some paranoid schizophrenic, just cuz she lives in your body.

15. So good, I'm in Minnesota and some redneck pig in a parka says, "Hey Judy, you're weird." Meanwhile, he sits near a hole in the ice for the next forty-eight days, waiting for some carp to jump up and say, "Eat me."

16. After I do a two-hour Judyism concert with my accordion, and some toad says, "Hey Judy, can you really play that thing?" No, Prince Happy Bladder, while you and your florist boyfriend were exchanging mood rings in the men's room, Lawrence Welk possessed me and now I'm just a hologram.

17. When I have to wake up at eight P.M. just to verbally abuse a herd of mortal swine.

18. Like I really need one more slug trying to make me spawn by saying he's a misunderstood genius with a terminal disease. That's like saying I should vote for Stalin just cuz he had jock itch. Right, fallout face, I can almost look at you without losing my hair. Count on it, Duke of Nuke.

19. Whole-earth-hog granola heads who say, "Hey Judy man, I don't put anything foreign into my body." Like I'm asking them to snort a Filipino.

20. So good, I'm trying to have a semi-nonnauseous meal at the International House of Perverts, and the waitress who looks like Jaba the Slut's afterbirth brings me my baked buffalo surprise. But before I even get a chance to sniff it she puts her grubby paws on it and barks, "Are you done yet?"

I say, "Excuse me, hog, but I'd like to taste it before you take it in back and wolf it down like a Banshee on food stamps."

She says, "Yeah, well, my shift is over, I want a tip."

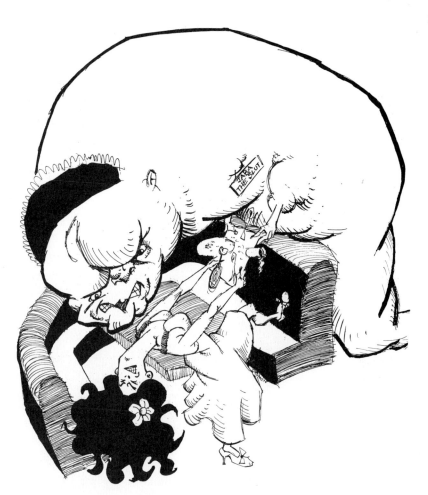

Fighting over my food with the waitress, Jaba the Slut.

So I say, "Plant your corn early, Pigolina." Tell me the government doesn't pay her ten thousand dollars a year not to release her cow eggs. Nice.

21. Life is so unfair. Why is it that your whole family can be wiped out from cancer before the age of five? There's one survivor, he comes home to watch TV, and the only thing on is the five hundredth annual Bob Hope "Sorry I'm Not Dead Yet" special.

22. So good, I love it when I'm staying at the Third World Motor Inn, relaxing all by myself in the hot tub, then twelve conventioneers in ten-gallon hats plop in and start making creme of potbelly soup. Real sanitary, squids.

23. Yuppie couples who give their kids names like Butt-bloat, then wonder why, when the kid turns five, he blows them away with a bazooka. If you want your kids to be really well adjusted, give them names that are distinctive but not disgusting. Like if you have twin girls, you should name them Jennifer Ann and Mr. Puss.

A Real Cop

24. I hate when a cop is not a real cop. It's one thing when a man is not a man or a woman is not a woman; the most they can do is beat you at tennis. But when a cop is not a real cop, he's a psycho pig pervert preying on petite flowers. Right, like I have time to let the Hillside Strangler stuff me into a Hefty trash bag and hide me in his trunk, just cuz he's too cheap to pay my way at the drive-in. The next time a car flashes a blue light in your rearview mirror, don't pull over, drive straight to K mart. If he's a real cop, he'll follow.

A Fake Cop

Pseudo-Virgins Who Spread Too Much

Are you constantly begging to be horizontal? When you meet a new stud puppet do you fantasize about shaving his head and using it as a giant roll-on deodorant?

Do you purposely seek out Attila the Hun types to beat you to a bloody pulp until you scream, "Thank you, sir, may I have another?"

Do you only date men named Oedipus or Alfred Lump?

When you accidentally brush up against a janitor in a crowded elevator, do you immediately rush out and get his name tattooed all over your buttocks?

Is his name Alfred Lump?

Do you insist on dating airline pilots who will pre-chew your food?

Are you a fat pig who wants to get even fatter so that Buzz Aldrin will rotate around you in a space capsule?

If you answered yes to any of the above questions, then you are a pseudo-virgin who spreads too much.

We all seek danger in our love relationships. How many times have you dated some squid because you were too lazy to commit suicide? So many Tupperware queens say, "Oh Judy, I've looked everywhere and I just can't find Mr. Right." Well, check the cemetery, slut. Why is it that a gorgeous fashion model with a Ph.D. in physics would marry a slime ape with a machete who reshapes her head into driftwood? Like my friend Maribeth Easy says, "Judy, I'm getting married. Will you come to my wedding?" Like I have time to buy her a blender just cuz some pipe fitter is poaching her eggs. Just cuz some busboy from Meals on Wheels found her F stop.

I said, "How do you know he loves you?"

And she says, "Cuz, he shot me in the head." Good logic, Barbie Braindead. While you're at it, why not have a pool party with Jerry Lee Lewis?

It's just like these born-again bimbos who can only be fulfilled by marrying a mass murderer. The warden says, "Hey, are you sure you wanna live with this guy? He brutally raped over eighty women."

And she says, "Well, that just proves he's a great lover." Right, psycho slut. Kind of a tip-off you're letting Ted Bundy drill you so you can be a giant media hog on Geraldo.

Then there are these broads who want to jump off a cliff because they can't get puffed. So they pay Mr. Spock twenty thousand smackers to implant into their wombs eggs fertilized by their ex-husbands so they can give birth to quints who look just like the dorks that dumped them. Really sharp, pop tarts.

Look, slutettes, if you just wanna be some pig's sock sniffer and butt groomer, why not spread for a slug who is at least rich and famous instead of unemployed and psychotic? If you must be a rib, be a rich one.

I am a goddess and living saint. But some women who have no lives, blond hair, and the ability to sponge, actually want to be mens' ribs and be hunted, pedicured, and mounted on a male mantelpiece next to Bullwinkle J. Moose. (Give me a quadrophonic break on that kind of fulfillment.)

But it takes a special kind of brainless troll to become a "rock rib." You know, the graduated groupie, the ex-model who is just begging to be horizontal for some millionaire anorexic guitarist (like there's any other kind), just to catch his sweat with her ruby-red-lipped, semi-nonvirginal orifice.

Examples? You want examples? Well, keep your prison pants on, Plankton. Don't pressure the healer of hermaphrodites. OK, so the archetypal rock rib would have to be Jerry Hall, the Texas model who puffed up twice for Mick Jagger and says that Mick is just a regular guy. Yeah, tell me she hasn't been reading Lewis Carroll. She even looks like a remedial Alice in Wonderland pushing a Gucci stroller. I'm sorry, love slaves, but I snuck into Mick Jagger's July '85 birthday bash at the Palladium in New York, where Mick was practically break-dancing on Jerry's very pregnant pouch. Yeah, Jer, that's about as regular as Herman and Lily Munster mating at a Mormon barbecue.

But I digress. I just had to mention Mick Baby's birthday. Do you mind, trogs? So far, there's Jerry Hall as the numer one rock rib. Now let's go back in time to Mick's ex, Bianca Jagger. Bianca is a borderline rock rib reject. She used to parade around as Mrs. Mick, but she proved to have a mind of her own, so that disqualifies this diminutive damsel. Besides, now she's leading a very altruistic lifestyle as a revolutionary fashion plate, fund-raising for Nicaragua.

Bianca was the mirror image of Mick; same build, same cheekbones, same ubiquitous mouth (look it up, slugs). Mick could look at her and see himself, but it frightened him because this self had a self of her own. Which brings me to Linda McCartney, Paul's pet, who is the mirror image of Paul himself, except blond, passive, and untalented, and therefore about as much of a threat as Ringo vocalizing at a Turkish bath. (These analogies don't always have to make sense, hogs.) However, Linda does have a special gift for singing "Ooh, ooh" in the background, while giving birth and gazing adoringly into her man's eyes. Tell me she didn't graduate from the Nancy Reagan/Babs Bush school of rib refinement.

Wait, I almost forgot about Margaret Trudeau. Remember her? She is the pseudo-virginal wife of Prime Minister Pierre, who did her husband and Canada proud by leaving him and their three offspring to throw herself at Mick Jagger's feet. Yeah, he almost noticed the WELCOME sign on your forehead. Good move, Mag. Now I hear you're teaching a course at NYU on supermoms and self-respect. Yeah, I'll be signing up for that one. Count on it, coquette.

But what about my personal favorite rock rib? That is none other than the inimitable (thank God) Yoko Ono. This impish artiste was facially the mirror image of John Lennon, who took over his mind and turned him into a bread-baking surrogate mom while she continued to sing (I use the term loosely) and invest his fortune in cows. (Like she almost had to leave home for that.) One can't help but love this Oriental "Cousin Itt," whose shrieks stir the souls of dead schnauzers. I even heard that some dinosaurs complained. Could you just hemorrhage, hogs?

Now that I have deified Jerry, Linda, Patti, Alana, Margaret, and Yoko, I'm throwing them all together to form the Rock Rib Band, also known as the Plastic Ono Band No. 2. So move over, Wilson-Phillips. The Rock Ribs will showcase on "Star Search" for Ed McMahon. (Yeah, I'm hot for you, Alpo king.) They will win as best spokes model sluts and will tour with Madonna, who is not a rock rib because she's too busy being Marilyn Monroe's rib. Yeah, I almost fell for that one, Mrs. ex–Pig Penn. Face it, video heads, Madonna is an armpit that got lucky. I mean it as a compliment.

Yoko being groomed by Emo.

Sports and Judyism

EVERY SPORT IS BASEBALL

In order to be a total love slave you must drain your brain of all thoughts, or else take up sports. I mean it as a compliment, Olympic oxen. First you must know that every sport is baseball and I can prove it. Let's go down the list, love leaches.

1. Bowling is baseball for morons, cuz you use the ball to hit the bats.
2. Tennis is baseball for yuppies, except it's a lot easier to hit one over the fence.
3. Golf is baseball for geriatrics, cuz all the outfielders are holes. (Once your sex slug reaches fifty, his idea of intercourse is putting his 9 iron on a golf green.)

4. Basketball is baseball, except you use the floor for a bat.
5. Dwarf tossing is baseball, but instead of pitching a ball, you toss Dr. Ruth. Perfect.

FOOTBALL MAKES YOU FAT

Don't get married, sex slugs, because once you're tied down to an exclusive love hog, you stop doing the most beneficial exercise in the known universe: husband hunting. Don't you see, you've enslaved your love leach in the bondage of matrimony, and he knows he has a full-time horizontal heifer, so he treats sex like taking out the garbage: he empties his Hefty bag once a week during "60 Minutes." Niice. The rest of the time, he plops in front of the TV and retains beer for the Super Bowl. By halftime he gives birth to a Miller Lite. So just to get his attention, you, the petite-flower wife, have to power-snort Cheetos until you look like the Astrodome.

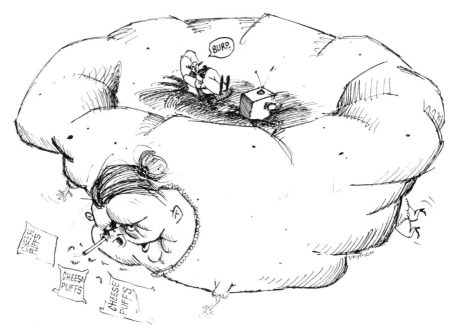

After marriage, a petite flower has to power-snort Cheetos until she looks like the Astrodome.

So . . . now that you're a stadium, he finally notices you. But instead of drilling you, he sits on you and inhales Crackerjacks and hot dogs. He can only get hard watching Mike Tyson pound a Panamanian into a pig skin. Perfect. So listen, married mutants, instead of watching football, *play it.* Then you'll both stay petite and plugged.

Tight ends grabbing each other's buns.

ICE HOCKEY AND LOVE HUNKS

❧

How does a petite flower, giver goddess, buffer of foreheads challenge her mind and stick-handle stud puppets? How else, trolls? By strapping in super-squid skates, grabbing a big fat macho hockey stick and smacking a puck with all the vengeance of a possessed pirate in a prom gown. That's right, trogs, I play hockey! The sport that lets a man go into combat and a woman be a wombat. But it's so much more than a sport; it's an art form, a ballet for frigid pachyderms. I mean it as a compliment, cogs. And for your information, TV drenched donkey enticers, hockey is the oldest sport known to man, next to primate pumping.

Let's go back in time, to the Ice Age, tundra toads, before Babs Bush sprouted one (deal with it, censors), when big, burly mastodons would go food gathering by using a frozen cave man as a stick and whacking a rock into the face of some unsuspecting slug, making him an instant Big Mac. It is no accident that today's Wayne Gretzkys look like the woolly mammoths of yesteryear doing an ice-mating dance. But these are fashion-slut woolly mammoths in elephant-man knee pads, bison boxer shorts, and loose-fitting rhino outerwear that can lead a petite flower like myself into sin, because I have to fantasize about what they look like underneath those polyester triceratops duds.

When these hot hockey hunks entice me with their slinky garb, I can't help myself—I want to release my eggs. So I, Judy, the Living Saint, go husband hunting on the ice and recruit new love slaves for Judyism.

Yes, I love hockey. But who was the wimped out, anal-retentive wuss who said hockey is violent? Poppycock. Hockey is est on ice. Besides, I can't stand those sissified sports like Ping-Pong; it sounds like Ling-Ling's G-string. Good move, Panda Putz. Keep your lily-livered soccer and thermonuclear war, give me twenty hulking slabs of meat on ice, begging to do my bidding. Not just regular sides of beef, but hulking hogs with no teeth and the collective IQ of a Tater Tot. Move over, West Virginia. All these ice puppets will then destroy false idols with a shot and a goal to slide on ice and become a Judy zombie. Ah, hockey, what perfect bondage.

How to Harness Cosmic Power Through Your Crotch

Yes, suburbanite slugs, you can possess the planet through your panties. What do you think Napoleon, Hitler, and George Michael have in common? That's right, irretrievably tight candypants. Oh sure, scholarly sissies keep harping on a good education, a better job, prestige, and respect. These things mean absolutely nothing without an activated crotch. Look at John F. Kennedy, Henry VIII, Cleopatra, and the Gabor sisters. They're all walking mattresses begging to be bounced on. Do you think any of them would have become half as famous if they were not superconductors of sex?

Be a whore and you'll get ahead. It's that simple. That's

why you haven't heard of me until now; my crotch was dormant. I was a petite flower who quickly became a tiger lily of the libido. If you want to be taken seriously, kiss up to every pig you meet, get some sturdy knee pads, and then put a liplock on their love muscle. Or else gain eight thousand pounds and bulldoze your way to power.

Remember, Alzheimer heads, you are exactly what you think all day long. Therefore, you are nothing. But now even nothings have hope.

Here is a letter:

Dear Judy, Divine Diva,
Because of your cosmic power slam dancing within me, I am now able to lift my once totally useless arthritic arm and surrender my wallet to you. Thanks for giving me a life in Judyism.

> *Signed,*
> *Tammy Faye Bakker*

Remember, all tragedies are opportunities in disguise. Let's say you lose your house, family, and your entire body in an earthquake because some city councilmen built a bridge out of Tonka toys. You can still thank God that you are not Oral Roberts so you don't have to beg the Almighty to send you the nine million bucks you spent on a George Jetson house with giant hula hands on the front lawn. Your only hope is to marry Alpo King Ed McMahon and then have him catch you in bed with a crossing guard. Then divorce him and look in your mail box; you may have already won millions from his death and dismemberment insurance. You see, in my religion, there are no problems, only solutions. Through Judyism you can become a healer instead of a heel. You can be the hero of your own life, not its victim.

You must take life by the hairy gonads and say "I'm gonna *squeeze* you with all the vengeance of a gay florist choking Anita Bryant until she becomes orange juice."

How, oh goddess, can I be all that I can be without joining the army? Simple. You must make Judyism your cosmos. Then you must set impossible goals for yourself and put even greater obstacles in your way so that you will never achieve them. Then and only then will you reach them.

Let's say you want to be the world's greatest long-distance runner. Experts say you must jog twenty miles a day and pump yourself up into a super-human running machine. Get yourself in the best physical condition possible, and eat only oats and barley. Wrong, Mr. Ed. If you really want to be the world's greatest runner, you should chop off your legs. That's right. Any baby can win a race with legs, but face it, gams are nothing but a physical crutch. You must propel yourself beyond the restraints of your body. Wouldn't it be a much greater achievement if you won the race as a human stump instead of big sissy dependent on limbs?

Let's say you wanted to be the world's most revered talk-show host. How would you go about it? Traditional TV executives would tell you to become a great speaker, learn to tell jokes, know your guests and make them feel comfortable. Wrong. Be a deaf-mute with no sense of humor who could care less if he has guests and then abuse and belittle them for showing up. Then you'd really get noticed.

Do not worry, warts. Worry is having more confidence in your problems than in my cosmic power to solve them. Worry is caused by a war between your ideal and your fear. Your ideal is to be President of the United States and boff every babe in sight. Your fear is that you will be caught. Don't worry, just become a Kennedy. So many people say, "Oh giver goddess, did JFK really have an affair with Marilyn?" Oh no, it's perfectly normal every time you climax to scream, "Ask not . . . what your country can do for you!" Just believe in your ideal and your fear will disappear. It could happen. Once I said to my boyfriend (OK, he's not

Judy the petite flower in performance.

really my boyfriend, but I needed a ride to the airport. *Is it so wrong?*), "Hey love squid, would you mind if I went out with other guys?"

He said, "No, why should I care?" And then a six-pound cantaloupe sprouted from his neck.

See? Don't bury your fears, admit them, androids. Don't repress, *express.* The next time some thoughtless thug offers to buy you a house, don't thank him, just look up from the sidewalk and say, "Excuse me, hog, does my cardboard box offend you, or what?"

Do you live your life in the future? Is the present a blur of anxiety about what you wish you were doing? Here is a love poem for no apparent reason. Eat it, apes.

I never want to be exactly where I am.
When I'm with you, I fantasize about Son of Sam.
It's just like heaven, hot waxing your hairy thighs.
But I'd rather be in prison being gang banged by
Biker guys.

So many syphilitic souls ask, "If Judyism is so great, why doesn't it wipe out war, famine, and death?" The answer is simple, slugs. I AM THE UNIVERSAL LOVE THANG. I RULE THE UNIVERSE THROUGH YOUR THOUGHTS. So stop thinking about AIDS and Nintendo, and fill your heads with nude rhino wrestling, and it will happen, hogs.

*T*he *G*oddess's *G*uide
to *M*ental *I*llness

As the matriarch of malcontents, I will teach you, slug puppet, how to go mental creatively.

Let's say you have a split personality. You can't decide whether you're a minister or a hooker; an astrophysicist or an ape. Well, Sybil, why not combine all your selves and become a channeler who charges movie stars millions of dollars to listen to one of your fake spirit voices. (Right, Ramtha, I really almost believe you're not doing your Elmer Fudd impression.)

If you have multiple personalities, become a channeler to the stars.

BULIMIA

Who's the big baby who says bulimia is unnatural? Right, Normalina, I'd like to see you down sixty pizzas and not throw up.

CATATONIA

Many mental cases (a euphemism for out-of-work actors), try to get attention by turning into rock formations. Sorry, toads, we already have one Mount Rushmore, but there's a casting call for headstones at Forest Lawn, so go plotz.

THE PARANORMAL

Do you know what the paranormal is? Look in your pants, pud. The paranormal is when similar events happen simultaneously. Like yesterday I ate breakfast, went outside, came in, ate lunch, went outside, came in, ate dinner, and went to bed. And the next day all that same stuff happened again. That's no accident, it's paranormal.

PARANOIA

So I'm driving down the expressway, and I have to apply my petite flower lip gloss, so I look in the rearview mirror . . . and I see all these cars right behind me. So don't tell me I'm not being followed. They cannot possess me, no.

Three Mystic Truths
for the Advanced Student
of Judyism

(Not for You Cheap Pigs Browsing in the Bookstore)

The meaning of these truths will be opened up to you only
if your heart is pure, your crevice is cleansed, and your
pocketbook is open. Meditate on them day and night, toad,
and their meanings will eventually reveal themselves unto
you. If not, sue me, Sasquatch.

SACRIFICE

Everyone exists solely to become an offering in the sacrifice
of Judyism. The world is an ever-burning fire. Feed that fire
with your sacrifice.

But don't you dare feed me raw dead fish—it's disgusting. I'm not your damn cat, so don't give me sardines or herring or ground-up anchovies—they're of the devil. Nasty.

The goddess is in your heart. Feed the goddess cheese corn and cherries jubilee.

ENERGY

Out of death comes life, and since I am the energy that supports all life, if you do not live through me, you are dead. And you know how much time you have to be dead, right? So use your life to live in Judyism.

DEATH IS FOR TROLLS

With Judyism, there is no death. Deceased loved ones are all around us, separated only by frequency. Your beloved is in the fourth dimension or the second dimension squared or a cartoon times itself. When your love thang croaks, he has submitted him or herself as a superzombie into the kingdom of Judyism. He is not dead; his bodily mass has been transformed into stud-puppet or pseudo-virgin energy. He could be a clapper or a Chia pet, or a television test pattern.

So the next time you get mad at your TV because it's only showing snow, or "Hee-Haw," don't turn it off . . . it could be your uncle Sludgie saying, "Hi."

*A*t *L*ast:
*Y*our *B*aptism into *J*udyism

Congratulations, pig! You have come this far and may now take the vow to become a full-fledged Judy zombie. You can administer it yourself. (As if I'm going to come over and swear you in personally. Dream on, tampon.)

After taking this vow, you will no longer be a worthless piece of crap with no reason to exist. You will be a worthless piece of crap that exists to worship me. Day and night, video heads who are still growing gills plead, "Oh great giver goddess, please spit on me and give my life meaning." Stop whining and repeat after me. Just do it, hog!

THE SACRED VOW OF JUDYISM

Realizing that I have no personality of my own or reason to live anyway, I do solemnly swear to keep the following tenets of my religion, Judyism:

I promise to continuously repeat Judy Tenuta's catch-phrases, such as, "It could happen" or "I am a pig in bondage for Judy," until my tongue falls off and/or I lose my job as sperm bank president.

I promise to name all of my children Judy the Petite Flower, even if they are human.

I promise to sell Judy's Giver Goddess Good Luck Sea Cow
Pendants on the freeway eighteen hours a day, and in return
Judy will give me four cents for food and a kick in the pants.

I promise to prepare and eat all of Judy's recipes, such as Judy's Anchovy Pudding, and Tex Tenuta's Barbecued Mule Muffins, even if this results in my looking like a senile ex-president.

I promise to save all my school lunch money to get plastic surgery to look as much like Judy Tenuta as a troll like me possibly can.

I promise to burn down my house and build a new one in
the shape of Judy's accordion, which I will then completely
wallpaper with her photos. And I will erect an altar in the
form of her boxer shorts, which will then become the focal
point of my useless existence.

I promise to violently attack, without one thought for my personal safety, any hog who refuses to worship Judy as a supreme goddess, be they animal, vegetable, and/or critic. I will kill them; I will maim them; I will destroy them; and then I will date them.

_____

(sign your name in duck's blood)

YOU ARE NOW A MEMBER OF THE SECRET ETERNAL
INTERNATIONAL MYSTIC LOYAL ORDER
OF JUDY ZOMBIES IN JUDYISM.
COULD YOU HEMORRHAGE, HOG?